MW01108026

Reading Matters 2

An Interactive Approach to Reading

Mary Lee Wholey

Continuing Education Language Institute
Concordia University

HOUGHTON MIFFLIN COMPANY   Boston   New York

Director of ESL Programs: Susan Maguire
Senior Associate Editor: Kathy Sands Boehmer
Editorial Assistant: Kevin M. Evans
Senior Project Editor: Carol Newman
Senior Production/Design Coordinator: Jennifer Waddell
Senior Manufacturing Coordinator: Marie Barnes
Marketing Manager: Patricia Fossi

Cover Design: Harold Burch Designs, NYC

www.hmco.com/college

Credits

Text credits p. 29: "How Drowsiness Shapes the Day," From *Sleep and Alertness: Chronobiological, Behavioral, and Medical Aspects of Napping,* David F. Dinges and Roger J. Broughton, eds. Copyright © 1989 Raven Press. Reprinted by permission of Lippincott-Raven Publishers. p. 88: Excerpt from, "Reasons for Buying Lottery Tickets," (11/5/97), Copyright © 1997 USA TODAY. Reprinted with permission. p. 102: Adapted from, "Currency on the Road," (7/7/97), Copyright © 1997 USA TODAY. Reprinted with permission. p. 113: "Interview with a Zoo Director," from "Playing God at the Zoo," by Jared Diamond. Copyright © 1992 Meredith F. Small. Reprinted with permission of Discover Magazine. p. 137: "Global Water Shortages," from "Global Water Shortages," by Mary H. Cooper. *CQ Researcher,* Dec. 15, 1995, Vol. 5, No. 47, pp. 1113–1136. Copyright © 1995 by Congressional Quarterly, Inc. Used with permission. p. 156: "With a Little Help from Her Friends" from NEWSWEEK, May, 29, 1995. Copyright © 1995 by Newsweek, Inc. All rights reserved. Reprinted by permission. p. 188: "The Lowdown on Handwriting Analysis," from "The Lowdown on Handwriting Analysis," by M. Scanlon and J. Mauro *Psychology Today,* November/December 1992. Reprinted with permission from *Psychology Today* Magazine. Copyright © 1992, Sussex Publishers, Inc.

Photo credits p. 3: © Bob Torrez/Liaison; p.15t: Andy LaValley. p.20b: N'Geven Tien/Gamma Liaison. p. 28: © Michael A. Dwyer/Stock Boston. p.41: Michael Newman/PhotoEdit; p.75: © Michael Newman/PhotoEdit. p.109: Fred Fellerman/Tony Stone Images. p.117: © Paul Vandevelder/Gamma Liaison. p.122: R.E. Barber. p.126: Art Wolfe/Tony Stone Images. p.151: © Tim Crosby/Gamma Liaison. p.156: Shonna Valeska. p.160: Gary Nylander/Kelowna Daily Courier. p.193: © Xinhua/Gamma Liaison. p.200b: Sygma. p.207: © Ken Marschall Collection. p.212: Woods Hole Oceanographic Institution.

Printed in the U.S.A.

Library of Congress Catalogue Number 98-72221

Student Book ISBN: 0-395-90427-7

2 3 4 5 6 7 8 9 – QF – 03 02 01 00 99

Contents

Introduction

The *Reading Matters* series is a four-level reading program comprised of texts at the high-beginning/low-intermediate, intermediate, high-intermediate, and advanced levels. This series combines stimulating readings with well-designed tasks that develop both fluency and accuracy at each level.

Extensive Reading

To develop fluency in reading, students need a significant amount of exposure to text, that is, extensive reading. Extensive reading provides the opportunity to develop automatic text processing skills. *Reading Matters* offers reading selections of sufficient length so that readers get the chance to increase the amount of time spent in silent reading. Variety in text types is an important element of extensive reading. The series features a variety of styles and genres so that readers develop an awareness of the scope of reading as well as the different purposes for which texts are written. Authentic texts or adapted authentic texts are used at appropriate levels.

Intensive Reading

Reading Matters features activities that help students develop fluency and accuracy in reading by activating two complementary text processing methods: top-down and bottom-up.

TOP-DOWN

Top-down processes are those that the reader applies to understand reading globally. Readers use their background knowledge of the topic and make predictions about what they expect to find out from reading. They confirm their predictions and begin to build a mental framework of the information in the reading selection. Awareness of rhetorical patterns—chronological ordering, cause and effect, and other discourse features—aids in the comprehension of information from reading. In addition, the activities in *Reading Matters* help to develop an awareness of a range of reading strategies, such as skimming, scanning, or previewing, that readers have at their disposal. The ability to apply these strategies appropriately is an important component of reading competency.

BOTTOM-UP

Knowledge of grammar and vocabulary has an effect on reading ability. Although readers can predict content from their knowledge of text structure or their background knowledge, a certain level of vocabulary recognition is required for processing text. *Reading Matters* introduces and develops vocabulary-building skills through activities such as guessing from context, recognizing meaning, grouping words, or identifying the use of special terms. In addition to a solid vocabulary, fluent readers have a good knowledge of syntactic structure. Actively examining the important grammatical features of a text provides a meaningful context for this kind of learning. To build reading competency, the amount of exposure to reading as well as the identification of and practice in the use of learning strategies for both vocabulary and grammar are tremendously important. *Reading Matters* provides direction to readers through activities in the *Vocabulary Building, Expanding Your Language,* and *Read On* sections.

Skills Integration and Interaction

Reading is an active process. Interaction between and among students helps facilitate this process. In exchanging ideas about the information in a text, readers confirm what they have understood. This confirmation process helps to develop accuracy in reading. It also provides a motivation for reading as well as a clear purpose in reading. Interaction with other students can best be accomplished when speaking tasks are an integral part of a reading activity and/or when the activity leads to the undertaking of writing tasks.

The interrelationship of skills integration and interaction requires a holistic approach to task design. The activities in *Reading Matters* are sequenced, and the recycling of tasks in different combinations allows the progressive development of reading competency in ways that offer challenge as well as variety. In *Reading Matters* the reader uses and reuses the language of the selection both implicitly to bolster an answer and explicitly in retelling the reading. Paired reading selections provide complementary or contrasting information on a topic. The readers orally explain the information from the reading they chose to those who read a different selection. Then, together they apply that information to carry out a new activity.

Text Organization

Reading Matters 2 contains six thematic units with three chapters in each unit on topics related to the themes. Two or three reading selections are featured in each chapter. The unit themes allow for topics of high interest to both academically oriented and general audiences. Most important, the selections are long enough for students to progressively develop fluency in reading. Through the chapter readings students are able to build a rich semantic network without sacrificing variety so that interest in the topic is not exhausted. Within each chapter, reading selections are structured so that the information from one selection can be contrasted and compared with another, allowing the students ample opportunity to discuss the points and counterpoints of the topic.

You can choose among the chapters of a unit to suit the needs of different program types and teaching approaches. Complexity in both text type and length, and difficulty in task type are structured to build gradually from chapter to chapter and unit to unit. Some overlap in level of language and task is built into each of the texts in the *Reading Matters* series so that you can accommodate the different reading levels of students within a class.

UNIT ORGANIZATION

Each unit in *Reading Matters 2* features the following sections:

- *Introducing the Topics.* This introductory section features the chapter opener photo and quote, and activities designed to stimulate the readers' curiosity about, prior experience with, or personal relevance to the theme. The tasks are interactive and draw on a variety of media: text, visual, and graphic.
- Each unit contains three chapters that present different topics loosely related to the theme.

CHAPTER ORGANIZATION

For each of the reading selections the following tasks are presented:

- *Chapter Openers* include pre-reading reflection through discussion questions, graphs, questionnaires, surveys, or illustrations. The purpose of this section is to stimulate discussion of key ideas and concepts presented in the reading and to introduce key vocabulary. Encourage students to explain their ideas as completely as possible. Teach students strategies for maximizing their interaction, such as taking turns, eliciting responses from all group members, naming a group leader and reporter. Whenever possible, re-form groups to give students a chance to talk more until they feel comfortable with the topic. Teacher–center at the end of this section and elicit key ideas and language from the students.

- *Exploring and Understanding Reading* contains content questions of differing levels of complexity, questions that guide students in the development of their reading strategies for improving general comprehension, for developing an awareness of text structure, and for evaluating the content of a text in detail. Emphasize the purpose of the activity and how it is tied to the development of a particular strategy. Help students to build up their tolerance for uncertainty. Point out that the purpose of comparing and checking their answers with the information in the reading is to verify as well as to become familiar with the information in the reading. Act as a resource to help students find the accurate information. An answer key is provided if and when it is needed.

- *Paired Readings: Recapping, Retelling,* and *Reacting to the Reading* are interactive activities that involve oral presentation of information from the readings, oral exchanges of information, and discussion that involves critical evaluation of ideas including comparison/contrast and debate. Help students to develop their ability to extract important information from a text by pointing out the purpose of and methodology for note-taking, highlighting, and underlining key information. Emphasize the importance of practice in order to explain the information in as natural and conversational a style as possible. Students can practice at home for in-class presentations.

- *Vocabulary Building* comprises tasks that introduce vocabulary building strategies such as the understanding of the interrelationship of grammatical structure and meaning, using context cues, and other aids to the fluent processing of reading selections.

- *Expanding Your Language* activities offer students other opportunities to use the material and strategies to help improve their own speaking and writing skills through further recycling of ideas from the readings. Tailor these activities to meet the needs of students who want more practice explaining information they read.

- *Read On: Taking It Further* provides opportunities for personal reading and related activities, including suggestions for further reading as well as reading and writing journal entries, vocabulary logs, and word play. While most of this work is done outside of class, time can be found in the class schedule to report on some of the activities. This gives students a purpose for the work and practice in developing their reading skills and strategies.

Acknowledgments

I am grateful to Susan Maguire who first suggested the idea for this series. Special thanks go to Kathy Sands Boehmer, who has been an invaluable help throughout the lengthy process of bringing this manuscript into its present form. Thanks also to Kevin Evans and the rest of the production and editorial staff at Houghton Mifflin Company.

My gratitude to the people who read the manuscript and offered useful suggestions and critical comments: Elinor Abdulla, University of Texas Pan–American, TX; Judie Bittinger; Sherrie Carroll, Montgomery College, MD; Susan Earle-Carlin, University of California, Irvine; Wendy Fero, American Language Academy, FL; Charles Garcia, University of Texas, Brownsville, TX; Barbara Hockman, City College of San Francisco, CA; Gail Kellersburger, University of Houston, TX; Barbara Lazzaro, ELS Language Centers, Seattle, WA; Jorge Perez, Southwestern College, CA; Laura Rossi-Le, Endicott College, MA; and Verna Sison, Seattle Central Community College, WA.

I would like to acknowledge the support and inspiring work of colleagues and students at the Continuing Education Language Institute (CELI) of Concordia University in Montreal. Special thanks go to Adrianne Sklar for her advice and suggestions after reading drafts of the material. The continuing support of Lili Ullman, Phyllis Vogel, and Nadia Henein has been invaluable to me. Thanks to Tanya Ullmann, who helped with the preparation of the Answer Key.

Finally, thanks to my family, Jerry, Jonah, and Yael, who haven't given up on me, even though they've heard "Can't right now, got to finish this work" for years on end.

Mary Lee Wholey

Reading Matters: Overview

UNIT	SKILLS	ACTIVITIES	VOCABULARY	EXPANSION
UNIT 1 Habits of a Lifetime	• predicting (1, 2) • previewing (1) • scanning (1, 2) • note taking (1) • getting the main idea (3) • using facts to make a case (3)	• categorizing (1) • evaluating information (1) • problem solving (1) • comparing stories (2) • answering a survey (3) • getting info. from a graph (3)	• using context to guess meaning (1) • sentence form (1) • synonyms (2) • antonyms (2) • word form (3)	• topic writing (1) • taking a position (2) • 2 minute taped talk (2) • tell and retell (3)
UNIT 2 Exploring Our Roots	• previewing an article (4) • getting the main idea (4) • scanning (4, 6) • note-taking (5) • personalizing (6) • relating main ideas and details (6)	• answering a questionnaire (4) • giving an opinion (4, 6) • categorizing (5) • recapping, reacting to, and retelling a story (5) • comparing stories (5) • applying the information: finding reasons (6)	• vocabulary in context; adjectives (4) • synonyms (4) • verb & preposition combinations (5, 6) • word form; roots (6) • using context to guess meaning (6)	• oral presentation (4) • role-play (5) • tell and retell (6) • topic writing (4, 6) • reacting to a story (5)
UNIT 3 Money Matters	• note-taking; categorizing (7) • scanning (8) • recognizing sub-points (9) • recognizing contrasting ideas (9)	• evaluating information (7) • problem solving (7) • survey (8) • recapping, retelling, and reacting to a story (8) • giving an opinion (9)	• expressions (7, 9) • advice sentence form (7) • matching meanings (8, 9) • vocab. in context; verbs (9)	• giving and getting advice (7) • survey (8) • discussing pro's and con's (9) • debate (9) • reaction writing (7, 9)
UNIT 4 Protecting Nature	• understanding explanations (10) • note-taking; advantages (10) • highlighting (11) • using facts to argue (11) • understanding details in extended example (12) • skimming a longer article (12) • scanning for specific facts (12) • previewing graphic information (12)	• adding examples (10) • making a decision (10) • giving opinions (12) • thinking about problems and solutions (12)	• jigsaw sentences (10) • word form; noun endings (11) • guessing meaning from context (12)	• writing about advantages (10) • writing your point of view (10) • summarizing and reacting (11) • 2-minute taped talk (11) • roleplaying an interview (11) • discussion (12)

Reading Matters: Overview *(continued)*

UNIT	SKILLS	ACTIVITIES	VOCABULARY	EXPANSION
UNIT 5 Personality	• chronology; following a story (13) • understanding descriptive detail (13) • recognizing sub-points and details (14)	• evaluating similarites & differences (13) • reacting to the story (13) • answering questions from notes (14) • making a chart to show results (14) • question making (14) • info-gap; reading diagrams (15) • applying information; evaluating the evidence (15) • reacting to information (15)	• expressions (13) • word forms; roots (13) • suffixes (13) • synonyms (14) • prefixes (15)	• personal writing (13) • 2 minute taped talk (14) • free writing (15) • oral presentation (15)
UNIT 6 The Search For Answers	• chronology; following a story (16) • understanding descriptive detail (16) • scanning for descriptive details (17) • finding main ideas (18) • using highlighting to make a list (18)	• question-making (16) • debating (16, 18) • note-taking; chronology (17) • making a timeline (17) • giving your opinion (17) • using illustrations to understand ideas (18) • note-taking; descriptive details (18) • theorizing (18)	• vocab. in context; verbs (16) • jigsaw sentences (16) • word forms (17) • descriptive language (17) • expressing possibility (18)	• 2 minute taped talk (16, 17) • role-play interviewing (18) • reaction writing (17) • writing a description (18)

Reading Matters 2

An Interactive Approach to Reading

Habits of a Lifetime

To Be Prepared Is Half the Victory
– MIGUEL CERVANTES

Introducing the Topics

The regular patterns of our life have an enormous effect on our feelings of happiness, success, and satisfaction in life. In this unit you will read about some of the habits that shape our lives. Chapter 1 is about how to structure study time. Chapter 2 is about the lifestyles of two people who have led long and interesting lives. In Chapter 3 there are some interesting facts about how our sleeping habits affect us.

Points of Interest

DISCUSSION QUESTIONS: HABITS

Think about these questions. Share your ideas with a partner or in a small group.

1. What are some common habits people have?
2. How do our habits affect our lives both positively and negatively?
3. Why do you think people try to change their habits?

COMMON EXPRESSIONS

Here are some sayings about habits. Discuss what each one means with a partner or in a small group. Try to agree on a meaning.

1. Good habits are so much easier to give up than bad ones.
2. Old habits die hard.
3. Make success a habit.

What sayings about habits do you know? Think of one to share with your classmates.

CHAPTER 1

Where Does the Time Go?

▨ Chapter Openers

What do you do to study effectively?

CATEGORIZING

Check (✔) a category for each of these activities.

■ *READING TIP:*
Thinking about a topic
before reading helps
you understand the
ideas more easily.

Activities	Study Skills	
	Good	Poor
1. Study in the library	✔	
2. Talk on the telephone		
3. Study in bed		
4. Do school work late at night		
5. Play music while doing schoolwork		
6. Study in a noisy place		
7. Study difficult subjects first		
8. Study when I am alert and focused		
9. Study when I feel tired and distracted		
10. Study with friends		

Compare answers with other students. You don't have to agree, but you should explain the reasons for your answers.

Exploring and Understanding Reading

PREDICTING

This reading is from a how-to textbook that gives useful information to help students become more successful in their studies and achieve their goals. What kind of information do you expect to find in a how-to book? Check (✔) the items you expect to find in the following list.

_____ Tips (Do's and Don'ts)

_____ Procedures to follow

_____ Long explanations about techniques

_____ Short explanations about techniques

_____ Short stories about different people's experiences

_____ Long stories about different people's experiences

Compare your choices with your partner's. Try to agree on your answers.

PREVIEWING

Writers use different types of headings and different types of graphics (for example, numbers or asterisks), to help the reader to get important information quickly. Some parts of the reading are in bold print or italics. By previewing special parts of the reading like graphics, titles, and subtitles, you can get a quick idea of the topic of a reading. As you preview, ask yourself these questions:

1. What kind of information will I get out of this reading?
2. What is the overall topic of this reading?
3. Who would be interested in this information?

Compare your answers with a partner.

Ways to Get the Most Out of Now

The following time management techniques are about when to study, where to study, ways to handle the rest of the world, and things you can ask yourself when you get stuck. As you read, underline, circle, or otherwise note the suggestions you think you can use.

When to Study

Be aware of your best time of the day. Many people learn best in daylight hours. If this is true for you, schedule study time or your most difficult subjects when the sun is up.

Many successful business people begin the day at 5 A.M. or earlier. Athletes and yogis use this time too. Some writers complete their best work before 9 A.M.

Some people experience the same benefits by staying up late. They flourish after midnight.

If you aren't sure what's best for you, experiment. When you need to study, get up early or stay up late.

Where to Study

Use a regular study area. Your body and your mind know where you are. When you use the same place to study, day after day, they become trained. When you arrive at that particular place, you can focus your attention more quickly.

Study when you'll be alert. In bed, your body gets a signal. For most students, it's "Time to sleep" and not "Time to study"! For that reason, don't sleep where you study. Just as you train your body to be alert at your desk, you also train it to slow down near your bed.

Easy chairs and sofas are also dangerous places to study.

Use a library. Libraries are designed for learning. The lighting is perfect. The noise level is low. Materials are available. Most people can get more done in a shorter time at the library. Experiment for yourself.

Ways to Handle the Rest of the World

Get off the phone. The telephone is the ultimate interrupter. People who wouldn't think of distracting you might call at the worst times because they can't see that you are studying. If a simple "I can't talk, I'm studying" doesn't work, then unplug the phone. Get an answering machine or study at the library.

Learn to say no. This is a time saver and valuable life skill for everyone. Many people feel it is rude to refuse a request. But saying no can be done effectively and courteously.

Avoid noise distractions. Avoid studying in front of the television and turn off the stereo. Many students insist they study better with background noises, and that may be true. Some students report good results with carefully selected music. A majority of research indicates that silence is the best form of music for study.

Schedule study sessions for times when your living environment is usually quiet. If you live in a resident hall, ask if study rooms are available. Or go somewhere else, where it's quiet, such as the library. Some students even study in quiet restaurants, laundromats, and churches.

Things You Can Ask Yourself When You Get Stuck

Ask: Can I do just one more thing? Ask yourself this question at the end of a long day. Almost always you will have enough energy to do just one more short task. The overall increase in your productivity might surprise you.

UNDERSTANDING DETAILS

Circle the letter of the correct answer. Underline the words in the reading that support your answer.

1. The author wants you to
   a. read carefully and remember all the ideas.
   b. read and underline or note useful suggestions.
   c. read and use all the suggestions.

2. Most people find they study best
   a. in the evening.
   b. after midnight.
   c. in the daytime.

3. The best place to study is
   a. in an easy chair.
   b. in bed.
   c. at a desk.

4. In the library most people can get
   a. more work done in less time.
   b. less work done in less time.
   c. the same amount of work done as usual.

5. When you study, it's best to have
   a. noise.
   b. silence.
   c. quiet music.

Compare answers with a partner. Look back at the reading if you disagree.

NOTE-TAKING: LISTING KEY WORDS AND PHRASES

■ *Reading Tip:* Note-taking is a useful way to make a record of the information you read. You can use notes to explain or write about what you have read. Remember to use only key words or phrases when you write notes.

Choose two of the study suggestions that you are interested in. List in note form the important information (i.e., the steps, benefits, or reasons) for the suggestions you chose. Look at the example to see how to make notes. Notice the key words and phrases. Compare these notes to the information in the reading.

Example: Use a library
  1. good lighting
  2. low noise level
  3. materials available
  4. get work done more quickly

A. _____   B. _____

1. _____   _____

2. _____   _____

3. _____   _____

4. _____   _____

5. _____   _____

TELLING AND RETELLING INFORMATION

■ *Retelling Tip:* When talking from notes, try not to read them. Look quickly at your notes to remind yourself of what you want to say. Then look at your partner and relate the information in a conversational way.

Step 1. Work with a partner who wrote about one of the same suggestions as you. Compare your notes orally. If you do not have the same or similar ideas on your lists, check the information in the reading.

Step 2. Work with a partner who prepared notes for a different suggestion and take turns explaining the information to each other.

After Reading

EVALUATING THE INFORMATION

Complete the information below. Then, share your ideas with a partner or in a small group.

From the reading and your experience, what study techniques do you think are the most difficult, the easiest, the least effective, and the most effective for you to use?

1. Most difficult _____

2. Easiest _____

3. Least effective _____

4. Most effective _____

Make a list of two or three techniques you agree in your group are the most important or effective. Present your group's choices to the class and explain the reasons for your choices.

APPLYING THE INFORMATION: PROBLEM SOLVING

1. Individual Work: What are three study problems that make it hard for you to succeed in your courses, for example, completing home-work assignments?

   a. List your study problems separately on a piece of paper.

   b. Give your papers to the teacher.

2. Group Work:

   a. Form small groups for problem solving.

   b. Your teacher will give each group a set number of problems to solve.

   c. Together discuss solutions to the problems you were given.

   d. Report your problems and solutions to the class.

Vocabulary Building

VOCABULARY IN CONTEXT

TIP: *Refer to the readings to help make your choices in the vocabulary activities.*

When you don't know the meaning of a new word, you can use the words you know to help you make a good guess. Use your understanding of the words or phrases in bold to help you guess the word that is missing.

Complete each sentence with one of the following words.

a. arrive d. discover g. lose i. surprise
b. ask e. experiment h. schedule j. train
c. complete f. increase

1. I worked at the library **for the first time** and was happy to

   _____ that I could do all my homework quickly.

2. It will _____ you to **discover** find out how much more you can do when you study early in the morning.

3. She had many **questions** that she wanted to

   _____.

4. She had to _____ all the work that was left **before she could go home**.

5. My friend was late and I **waited over an hour** for him to

   _____ at the library.

6. I'll **check my agenda** to see if we can _____ a time to get together and finish the project.

7. I decided to _____ by **getting up at different times** until I found the best time to study.

8. It takes **time and willpower** to _____ yourself not to answer the phone when it rings.

9. The **answering machine is on** because I don't want to

   _____ study time talking on the phone.

10. You can _____ your productivity by **getting up fifteen minutes earlier than you normally would every day**.

Work with a partner and take turns reading the completed sentences.

SENTENCE FORM

Tips are often written in the form of a command to do or not do something. The sentence usually begins with a verb. Scan the readings and find five sentences that start with a verb and give suggestions or commands.

Example: <u>Practice</u> these new time management techniques.
          verb

Write the sentence. Underline the verb.

1. _____

2. _____

3. _____

4. _____

5. _____

Work with a partner and take turns reading your sentences.

Expanding Your Language

TOPIC WRITING

Write about some study habits that are important to you based on your discussion and the chapter readings. To do this, follow these steps.

1. Outline the ideas about each habit.

   Study Habit 1: _____   Study Habit 2: _____

   What _____   What _____

   How _____   How _____

   _____   _____

   _____   _____

   Why _____   Why _____

   _____   _____

   _____   _____

2. Write two or three sentences about *the habit*.
3. Write three or four sentences about *how* to follow it.
4. Write three or four sentences about *why* it is important.
5. Write about each habit in a separate paragraph.

In writing, remember to do the following:

- Indent at the beginning of the paragraph, as in this example:

  There are three main study techniques that I think are important for being successful in school.

- Explain the ideas in complete sentences. In English a sentence usually has a subject, a verb, and an object.

  Many students unplug their phones.
  subject   verb   object

CHAPTER 2

Habits of a Lifetime: Are We Affected?

■ Chapter Openers

DISCUSSION QUESTIONS: LIFESTYLES

Think about these questions. Share your ideas with a partner or in a small group.

1. a. What habits can lead to a long life?
   b. What habits might shorten your life?
2. Are people's lives today easier or more difficult than they were in the past?
3. How would your life change without modern conveniences like indoor plumbing or electricity?

PAIRED READINGS

These are the stories of two women who have lived long and interesting lives. Imagine you were preparing to meet someone who was much older than you and who had lived through difficult times. What would you expect them to tell you?

PREDICTING

Write down (in a few words) what you expect to read about in these stories. List as many ideas as you can. The first idea is given as an example.

1. I expect to read about their . . .

2. <u>experience of historical events</u>

3. _____

4. _____

5. _____

Choose one of the stories. Work with a partner who is reading the same story.

■ ■

Reading 1: A Life Well Lived

UNDERSTANDING DETAILS

Read the story and then look for the answers to the questions after each paragraph. Underline the words in the paragraph that support your answers.

A.   Birdle Mannon is 87 and lives in a one-room wood house built by her father in the woods near the village of Brownbranch, forty miles away from Springfield, Missouri. She doesn't have electricity, running water, or indoor plumbing. She heats her house and cooks her food on a wood stove that she keeps supplied by cutting her own wood. She collects rainwater to use for cooking, bathing and washing her clothes. When she needs to, she uses an outhouse that she built down the path from her house. She cooks her own food from a few supplies that she buys in the village. She keeps food cold in a special underground cellar next to her house. The year is 1997 but her life is not very different from the way it was when she first came to this place with her family in 1916.

1. Where does Birdle Mannon live?

   _____

2. How does Birdle heat her home?

   _____

3. Where does she get her water?

   _____

4. When did she first come to her home?

   _____

5. How are her home and her life similar to the way they were when she first came there?

   a. _____

   b. _____

   c. _____

   d. _____

B.   Birdle came to Missouri with her parents, her brother and two sisters in 1916 when she was six years old. They came because they heard that there was good land and lots of water available for farming. Mr. Mannon bought 120 acres of land for $800. It was autumn when the family arrived and Birdle's father quickly built a tiny wood house for protection before winter arrived. Birdle remembers sleeping on the floor while the house was being built. The family was poor. Birdle's father worked hard to raise crops like corn and oats, chickens and cattle to survive. Times were not easy. One of Birdle's sisters died in the flu epidemic of 1918. Her brother died in 1926 and her father died in 1936. The Mannons acquired only a few modern conveniences. They had a pick-up truck, a portable radio, and in 1970 they got a telephone installed. After her mother died in 1969 and her sister in 1972, Birdle was left alone and had to manage on her own.

1. How old was Birdle when she came to her home?

   _____

2. Why did her family come to Brownbranch, Missouri?

   _____

3. a. How much land did Birdle's father buy?

   _____

   b. How much did the land cost?

   _____

4. What did Birdle's father do to support the family?

   _____

5. What happened to Birdle's family?

   _____

6. What happened to Birdle after 1972?

   _____

C.   Birdle decided to stay in her house in the woods, but not because she didn't have other opportunities in life. She had gone to college and trained to be a teacher. She taught school in two of the villages near her home. She also taught Sunday school at the local church and wrote local news reports for two area newspapers. Birdle chose to stay in her home because, as she says, "This is the place where I belong." Birdle's attitude is that a person can't do everything in life, so do what makes you happy. She may not have an easy life, but she has kept busy. Some people in the community worry that at 87 Birdle is too old to be living by herself. Her neighbors try to help her. They stop in to bring her to the village store for groceries or to bring her to church on Sunday. Birdle is glad for the help from her neighbors but she's not yet ready to leave her house in the woods. As she says, "I can still cut my own wood and pump my own water. In my mind and heart, I don't feel old." She is living proof of the saying "Old habits die hard."

1. What facts show that Birdle could have lived a different kind of life?

2. What is her attitude toward life?

3. Why do Birdle's neighbors worry about her?

4. How does Birdle feel about living in the woods at her age?

Compare answers with your partner. Try to agree on the same answer. Look back at the reading if you disagree.

RECAPPING THE STORY

Work with a partner who read the same story. Reread the first paragraph quickly. Cover the information and tell your partner as much as you can remember. Ask for help if you forget or give incorrect information. Take turns reading and telling the information in all the paragraphs.

REACTING TO THE STORY

Discuss these questions with a partner.

1. a. Would you ever choose to live the way Birdle does?
   b. What would you like about it, and what would you miss?
2. Do you think that Birdle can continue to live on her own? Why or why not?
3. Do you agree with Birdle's attitude toward life? Why or why not?

Reading 2: The Secrets of a Long Life

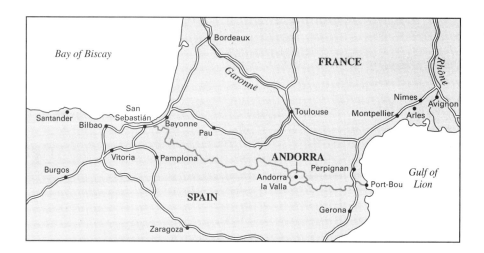

UNDERSTANDING DETAILS

Read the story and then look for the answers to the questions after each paragraph. Underline the words in the paragraph that support your answers.

A. Jeanne Calment holds the record for being one of the world's oldest people. When she died in 1997, she was 122 years of age. Many people were curious about this unusual woman. Reporters asked her about her memories. Calment could remember meeting the painter, Vincent Van Gogh, at a local store in 1888. She told reporters that she thought he was a grouchy and disagreeable man. Reporters often asked her to tell them the secret of her long life. She would just shrug and say, "Maybe God has forgotten me." People asked her a lot of questions about the details of her daily life. Perhaps they hoped that they could find the key to living a long and active life by finding out about her daily habits.

1. Who was Jeanne Calment?

   _____

2. When did she die?

   _____

3. What did people ask her about?

   a. _____

   b. _____

4. Why did people want to know about the details of her life?

   _____

B.   Jeanne lived in Arles, a city in southern France, where she was born in 1875. She was born into a middle-class family and lived an ordinary life. She married and had a daughter. Unfortunately, her husband, her daughter, and an only grandson all died before her, leaving her to live alone. Her eating habits were not especially healthy. She ate chocolate almost every day. In fact, she once estimated that she ate about a kilogram of chocolate a week. She liked to smoke and she smoked cigarettes until she was 117 years old. She also liked to drink a glass of wine with her noon meal. She took care of her physical appearance, regularly rubbing her skin with olive oil. She was an active woman and rode a bicycle until she was 100 years old. She took a brisk, long walk every day. On her 100th birthday she even walked all over the city to thank different people for wishing her a happy birthday.

1. Where did Jeanne spend her life?

_____

2. What sad events happened in her life?

_____

3. What habits did she have?

    a. _____

    b. _____

    c. _____

    d. _____

4. What kind of physical activities did she like?

    a. _____

    b. _____

C. Many people asked Calment to tell them her secrets for living a long life. Certainly, her family history must have played some part; her mother lived to be 86 and her father lived to be 93. But, people who knew Calment suggest that the secret lies in the make-up of her personality. Friends said that she didn't seem to worry too much. She didn't appear to suffer from stress. She had a positive attitude toward life. She said, "If you can't do anything about it, don't worry about it." She was the kind of person who looked for things in life to smile about. In her later years she couldn't see or hear people because she had become deaf and blind. In spite of that, she still felt that she had something to be happy about every day.

1. What was important about Jeanne Calment's family history?

    _____

2. What was her attitude toward life?

    _____

3. a. What physical problems did Jeanne have?

    _____

    b. How did they affect her attitude toward life?

    _____

Compare answers with your partner. Try to agree on the same answer. Look back at the reading if you disagree.

RECAPPING THE STORY

Reread the first paragraph quickly. Cover the information and tell your partner as much as you can remember. Ask for help if you forget or give incorrect information. Take turns reading and telling the information in all the paragraphs.

REACTING TO THE STORY

Share your ideas about these questions with a partner.

1. What do you find interesting about this woman's life?
2. What habits do you think helped this woman to live a long life?
3. What do you think is the secret to living a long life?

After Reading

COMPARING THE STORIES

1. Work with a partner (or partners) who read a different story. Tell your partner the details of the story you read. Then, listen to your partner's story. Discuss the similarities and differences between these stories.
2. Discuss the questions in the "Reacting to the Story" section for both stories.
3. Make a list. What are the lessons for living long and fulfilling lives in these two readings? Be prepared to share your list with others in the class.

GIVING YOUR OPINION

What do you think has the greatest influence on our chances for a long and fulfilling life? List five things that influence our chances to live long and happy lives. Number your ideas from most (1) to least (5) important.

1. **Example:** positive attitude

2.

3.

4.

5.

Work with a partner or in a small group. Try to agree on the factors and, if possible, on their order of importance. Report the results to your classmates.

Vocabulary Building

SYNONYMS

Circle the word that has the closest meaning to the word in boldface.

1. **heat**   make   prepare   warm   serve

2. **protection**   safety   building   floor   supplies

3. **produce**   provide   make   speak   use

4. **curious**   glad   active   questioning   ready

5. **attitude**   outlook   habit   proof   opportunity

6. **active**   happy   physical   busy   passive

7. **deaf**   unhearing   unseeing   unbelieving   unusual

8. **brisk**   slow   sudden   fast   poor

Write three sentences using words from the list.

1. _____

2. _____

3. _____

ANTONYMS

Antonyms are two words that have opposite meanings, like good and bad. Match the word in Column A with its antonym in Column B.

Column A   **Column B**

_____ 1. happy   a. far

_____ 2. quickly   b. negative

_____ 3. positive   c. short

_____ 4. smile   d. slowly

_____ 5. different   e. forget

_____ 6. near   f. frown

_____ 7. old   g. similar

_____ 8. long   h. young

_____ 9. remember   i. sad

Write three sentences using words from the list.

1. _____

2. _____

3. _____

■ Expanding Your Language

WRITING

Take a position: In the future, people will live longer. Write your opinion about the following question:

What do you think are the most important things people should do if they want to live a long and fulfilling life?

Go back to the exercises in the section After Reading on page 24. Use the information from these exercises and discussions you've had to help focus your ideas.

1. Write a list of ideas. For each idea, think of some facts, examples, stories, or other information of your own.

Example:

A. To live a long life

Idea 1: Be active

- Walk every day (Jeanne Calment)

- _____

Idea 2: _____

- _____

- _____

B. To live a fulfilling life

Idea 1: Have a positive attitude

- Don't worry about yesterday's problems, do something good today

- _____

Idea 2: _____

Do this work in your journal notebook.

2. Work with a partner and explain your ideas to each other. Help each other to add to the list of ideas.
3. Write your ideas in complete sentences. Indent at the beginning of each paragraph.
4. Give your final writing to your teacher.

SPEAKING

Two-Minute Taped Talk: Record a two-minute audiotape about one of the stories in this chapter.
  To make your tape, follow these steps:

1. Write some notes about the important information in the story.
2. Practice telling the story from your notes. Include as many important facts as possible.
3. Time yourself as you try to speak as clearly and naturally as possible.
4. Record yourself telling the story.
5. Give the tape to your teacher for feedback.

CHAPTER 3

The Power of Naps

Chapter Openers

DISCUSSION QUESTIONS

Think about these questions. Share your ideas with a partner or a small group.

1. Do you feel sleepy during the day? At what times?
2. What do you do to "wake up" when you feel sleepy?
3. If you could, would you take a nap during the day?
   a. When?
   b. For how long?
   c. Where?
4. Do you think that taking a nap is a sign of laziness? Why or why not?

INFORMATION FROM A GRAPH

Read the graph and get information from it to answer these questions.

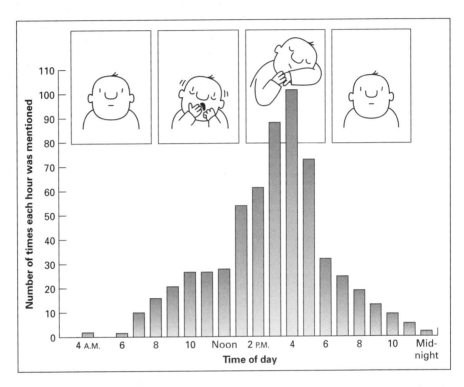

Two hundred seventy-six young adults reported that they feel sleepy most often in the middle of the afternoons.

1. When did people in this study say they felt the most tired?

   _____

2. How many times did people say they felt tired at:

   2 P.M. _____

   9 A.M. _____

   6 P.M. _____

3. What could be some reasons more people feel tired at 4 P.M. than at 6 P.M.?

Exploring and Understanding Reading

PREDICTING

This reading contains some factual information and advice about our need for sleep. You can more easily understand the reading by thinking about what happens to you when you get tired.

CATEGORIZING

Check (✔) the things that people might do when they feel tired. Add two ideas of your own.

_____ 1. Forget a person's name.

_____ 2. Forget to do something important.

_____ 3. Solve a difficult problem.

_____ 4. Work an extra shift or work overtime.

_____ 5. Make a bad decision.

_____ 6. Get angry with a friend.

_____ 7. _____

_____ 8. _____

Work with a partner to compare your choices.

■ ■
We Need to Nap!
■ ■

A. Do you ever feel sleepy during the day? Researchers into sleep have found some interesting facts about our body's natural sleep rhythms. There are two points during a 24-hour period when people most feel the need to sleep. These times are the hours between 1 and 4 P.M. during the day and between 1 and 4 A.M. in the morning. One study of 276 young adults showed that people have the most difficulty staying awake between two and five o'clock in the afternoon and in the morning. These are also the hours when there are increases in traffic accidents causing death. Being tired affects your ability to think and make decisions. You forget more easily and feel less alert. You have slower reaction times. In addition, fatigue affects our mood and outlook on life.

B. North Americans seem to be cutting down on the number of hours they sleep. In many countries, people stop their work in the afternoon and have a nap. But, in countries like Canada and the United States, business continues all day long. In North America, the number of people who work for 10–12 hours a day is increasing. More people are working overtime. More people are working night shifts, from 11 P.M. until 7 A.M. But most adults need about 7–10 hours of sleep a day. On average, North Americans are only getting about 6–8 hours of sleep. In fact, over the past century, North Americans have reduced the number of nightly sleeping hours by about 20 percent.

C. Some experts are worried that tired workers are becoming a danger in the workplace. A tired worker is likely to forget important information and make mistakes. Mistakes can lead to serious work accidents. Tiredness has been linked either directly or indirectly to some of the worst accidents in history like the nuclear accidents at Three Mile Island, as well as the explosion of the space shuttle *Challenger*. Allowing workers to nap could help solve the problem. Research into allowing people in the airline industry to take short naps is producing some interesting results. Researchers at NASA have studied the effects of taking 40-minute naps for pilots on overseas international flights. They found that when pilots napped, they were more alert afterward. Their reactions were 16 times faster than crew members who hadn't napped.

D. Sleep researchers have some advice for people who want to make a habit of napping in the afternoon.

What To Do:

- Take a nap at the time when your body most needs to sleep: eight hours after getting up and eight hours before your bedtime at night.
- Take a nap every day even if you don't feel tired.
- Remind yourself that taking a nap is not a sign of laziness.
- Find a place to lie down to nap.
- Shut off your phone or close the door so that you won't worry about being disturbed.
- Take a minute to breathe slowly and relax your body before closing your eyes.
- Nap for 15–20 minutes. Try not to nap for longer than 30 minutes.
- After you wake up, move slowly for a few minutes. Don't try to move into action quickly.

GETTING THE MAIN IDEA

Read the list of main ideas. Write the main idea for each of the paragraphs on the correct line.

MAIN IDEAS

Some advice for people who want to take a nap in the afternoon.
The decrease in the amount of time people are sleeping.
Some information about our body's natural sleep rhythms.
The problem of tired workers and some solutions to this problem.

Paragraph A. _____

Paragraph B. _____

Paragraph C. _____

Paragraph D. _____

SCANNING: GETTING THE FACTS

A. Circle T for true or F for false. Underline the information that supports your answer.

1. T   F   More people feel tired at 4:00 P.M. than at 10:00 in the morning.

2. T   F   There are more traffic accidents at four o'clock than at six o'clock.

3. T   F   Fatigue can make people moody.

4. T   F   People in the United States and Canada are getting more sleep than in the past.

5. T   F   Fatigue causes accidents at work.

B. Circle the correct choice in each sentence. Underline the information in the reading that supports your answer.

1. In North America people **are** / **aren't** in the habit of taking a nap.

2. In many countries people **do** / **don't** work all day.

3. In North America **more** / **fewer** people are working night shifts.

4. Our bodies have **one** / **two** periods when we feel the need to sleep the most.

5. Many Americans **do** / **don't** feel tired during the day.

6. Pilots who napped had **faster** / **slower** reactions in carrying out their work.

Compare answers with a partner. Try to agree on the same answer. Look back at the reading if you disagree.

After Reading

IN-CLASS SURVEY

Answer these questions for yourself. Interview two others in your class. Write their answers in note form.

1. a. During the day, do you feel tired?

   Yes   No

   Often   Sometimes

   Never

   b. If yes, at what time of the day do you feel tired?

2. How many hours do you usually sleep?

   4–6   6–8   8–10

3. When do you usually go to bed?

4. When do you usually get up?

5. a. Do you ever take a nap during the day?

   b. If yes, when do you take a nap? For how long?

6. Is it a good idea for people to take naps at work? Explain the reasons for your answer.

   Yes   No   Why?

Discuss your answers with a partner. Did people answer the questions similarly or differently?

APPLYING THE INFORMATION: USING FACTS TO MAKE A CASE

Read the short article that follows and then discuss this question: Why were these workers suspended from their jobs?

▪▪ *Surprise Inspection at Area Schools Yields Results* ▪▪

Six school caretakers have been told to leave their work for napping on the job. The suspensions were given to six workers. They will have from one week to one month without pay. School supervisors carried out the surprise checks last week. They found one worker sleeping under a blanket with a pillow under his head. Another worker had an alarm clock to wake him an hour before the end of his work. Three workers were caught taking a group nap. The school board chairman said that they have had problems with workers sleeping during the night shift for a number of years. But they decided to get serious and deal harshly with the problem only recently. The school board announced that they hoped this would be the last time they hear of this kind of problem. The chairman stressed that, while workers who sleep on the job represent only a small percentage of the total number of employees, the suspensions would discourage anyone who feels the need to sleep on the job. "I don't think it's too much to ask that, when we pay them good salaries to do the job," he said. Staff members must remain alert to know if vandals are breaking into the schools to steal from or cause damage to the schools.

UNDERSTANDING DETAILS

What are the facts of this case? Underline the important facts in the article: What happened? To whom? Why? When? What was the result? Work with a partner and talk about the facts of the case.

1. Do you think that these workers should be suspended?
2. Do you think the suspensions will solve the problem? Based on the ideas in the first chapter reading, what other solutions could you suggest?

Work with a partner or in a small group and present your ideas. Try to reach agreement. Prepare to present your ideas to others.

Vocabulary Building

WORD FORMS

In English, the form of a word can change when it is used as a different part of speech. In these sentences you will decide if you need a noun (an idea or a thing) or an adjective (a word that describes an idea or a thing).

Choose the correct word to complete the sentences.

1. sleep / sleepy

    a. My need for _____ was affecting my ability to get my work done.

    b. I felt _____ even though I had gone to bed at 9:00 P.M.

2. mood / moody

    a. She didn't like to be with him when he was _____.

    b. He didn't want to stay because she was in a bad _____.

3. day / daily

    a. I work eight hours every _____, six days a week.

    b. Her _____ routine was always changing.

4. difficulty / difficult

    a. It's _____ to concentrate when you feel tired.

    b. She had _____ with the schedule.

5. night / nightly

    a. She liked her _____ routine of reading the newspapers.

    b. She didn't like to work at _____ because she felt tired the next day.

Work with a partner and take turns reading the completed sentences.

SYNONYMS

Match the word in Column A with its synonym in Column B.

Column A   **Column B**

_____ 1. continue   a. stop for a period of time

_____ 2. alert   b. response to an action

_____ 3. benefit   c. go on for a period of time

_____ 4. reduce   d. advantage

_____ 5. surprise   e. decrease

_____ 6. suspend   f. feeling awake and lively

_____ 7. fatigue   g. feeling inactive

_____ 8. lazy   h. the study of a problem

_____ 9. reaction   i. feeling of tiredness

_____10. research   j. without warning

Expanding Your Language

SPEAKING

A. **Tell and Retell:** Quickly reread the tips for what to do if you want to take a nap. Work with a partner. Cover the information and take turns giving as many tips as you can remember to each other.

B. **Two-Minute Taped Talk:** What are your sleep habits? Have they changed in the last few years? Do you need to get more sleep or are you getting enough? Do you ever feel sleepy?

Using your own ideas and the information in this chapter, prepare a two-minute taped talk about these questions or any of your own ideas on the topic of sleep and naps. Prepare your ideas before you record. Make a short outline of your ideas in note form. Practice your talk a few times before you record. Record your talk and give it to your teacher for feedback on content and clarity of ideas.

WRITING

Topic Writing: Write about the topic of your taped talk. Follow the instructions on page 13.

Read On: Taking It Further

Researchers have found that the more you read, the more your vocabulary will increase and the more you will understand. A good knowledge of vocabulary will help you to do well in school and in business. To find out more about your reading habits, answer the following questionnaire.

READING QUESTIONNAIRE

Rank the activities that you think help you to increase the amount of vocabulary you understand. Mark (1) beside those that help you the most to learn new vocabulary, (2) beside the second, and so on. Mark the same number if you find two activities that help you equally.

_____ Memorizing word lists

_____ Reading texts that are assigned for class

_____ Reading texts that I choose for myself

_____ Talking about the texts that we read for class

_____ Talking about the texts that I choose for myself

_____ Learning how to guess the meaning of words that are new

_____ Doing vocabulary exercises for reading that we study in class

_____ Doing extra vocabulary exercises for homework

_____ Studying the dictionary to find out the parts of words

_____ Using the dictionary to look up new words I don't understand

Discuss your questionnaire with a partner. Do not worry if your answers are different from your partner's. Explain the reasons for your ranking and your experiences with reading. Are there other activities you find help you to increase your vocabulary?

A READING JOURNAL

■ *READING TIP: Keep a notebook to write your reading journal and vocabulary log entries.*

An important way to improve your reading skills and increase your vocabulary is to find material that you choose to read. This activity is called "reading for pleasure." Here are some ideas to start you out.

READING

Find some readings on the topics in this unit that you are interested in and that are at your level. For example, you could find an easy reading edition of "Rip Van Winkle" by Washington Irving. This is the story of a man who took a very long nap. Another source of reading material is your bookstore or library's magazine and newspaper section. Make a schedule for a time when you plan to do your personal reading. Discuss what you would like to read with your teacher and with others in a small group. Your teacher can help you to find some material to read for your pleasure. Your group members could recommend something good for you to read.

WRITING

At the end of each week complete a journal report about what you read. Explain the important ideas and what you learned from this reading. Write about what you liked or found interesting. Explain whether or not you would recommend the reading to others.

SPEAKING

Each week, be ready to talk about what you read with a partner or with others in a small group. You can use your journal report to help you to recall what is important for the others to know.

READING JOURNAL REPORT

Include the following information in your journal entry:

Title of the reading: _____

Author: _____

Subject of the reading:

_____

_____

_____

_____

Summary of the important ideas:

_____

_____

_____

_____

Personal reaction:

_____

_____

_____

_____

Recommendation:

_____

_____

_____

VOCABULARY LOG

Choose five important words that you learned in each chapter. Write the words and your definition in your notebook. Check your definition with the teacher.

Example:

CHAPTER 1	WORD	DEFINITION
1.	benefits	some good points
2.		
3.		
4.		
5.		

WORD PLAY: A SPELLING GAME

You can use vocabulary from the chapter readings to play this game. Think of a pair of words, like *paid* and *distract*. The last letter of *paid* is the first letter of *distract*. Select a partner and follow these rules to play the game.

1. Make a list of seven to ten words from the readings that can be paired with another word.
2. Give your partner the first word to spell.
3. Your partner spells the word and then must select a new word that begins with the last letter of the word spelled (time limit: one minute). If your partner can't find a word, you supply an answer.
4. Continue to take turns until the teacher calls time (after approximately ten to fifteen minutes)
5. The person who correctly chooses and spells the most words wins.

UNIT 2

Exploring Our Roots

If the Roots Are Solid, the Tree Will Grow Strong

—S. WEIL

Introducing the Topics

In this unit you will read about one of the fastest-growing interests in North America—genealogy. Looking into our family history is the third most popular hobby in the United States. Chapter 4 is about the customs and traditions of choosing names. Chapter 5 explores the reasons that people decide to research their roots. In Chapter 6 you will read about autobiography writing and find out why people write about their past.

Points of Interest

DISCUSSION QUESTIONS: FAMILY HISTORY

Think about these questions. Share your ideas with a partner or in a small group.

1. Did you ever try to find out about the past history of your family? If yes, what did you learn? If no, what would you like to learn?
2. Why is it important to tell family stories from one generation to the next?
3. What interesting stories do you know about your family or about families in your country?

FAMILY TREE

Complete as much of this chart as you can. Show the chart to a partner and use it to talk about some of the people in your family. If possible, bring photographs of family members.

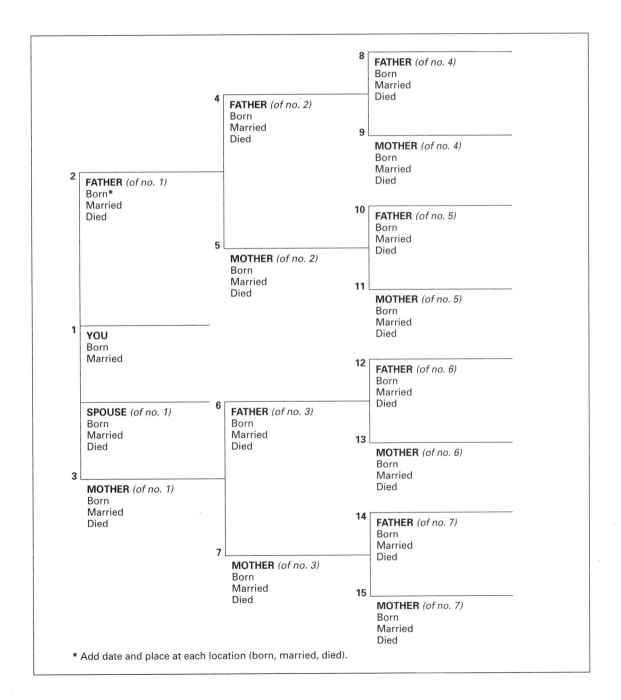

8 **FATHER** *(of no. 4)*
Born
Married
Died

4 **FATHER** *(of no. 2)*
Born
Married
Died

9 **MOTHER** *(of no. 4)*
Born
Married
Died

2 **FATHER** *(of no. 1)*
Born*
Married
Died

10 **FATHER** *(of no. 5)*
Born
Married
Died

5 **MOTHER** *(of no. 2)*
Born
Married
Died

11 **MOTHER** *(of no. 5)*
Born
Married
Died

1 **YOU**
Born
Married

12 **FATHER** *(of no. 6)*
Born
Married
Died

SPOUSE *(of no. 1)*
Born
Married
Died

6 **FATHER** *(of no. 3)*
Born
Married
Died

13 **MOTHER** *(of no. 6)*
Born
Married
Died

3 **MOTHER** *(of no. 1)*
Born
Married
Died

14 **FATHER** *(of no. 7)*
Born
Married
Died

7 **MOTHER** *(of no. 3)*
Born
Married
Died

15 **MOTHER** *(of no. 7)*
Born
Married
Died

* Add date and place at each location (born, married, died).

CHAPTER 4

What's in a Name?

Chapter Openers

DISCUSSION QUESTIONS: WHAT'S IN A NAME?

Think about these questions. Share your ideas with a partner or in a small group.

1. What is the origin or meaning of your first name?
2. What do you know about the history of your family name?
3. Would you ever change your name? What are some reasons why people change their names?
4. What names do you like?
5. What are some common nicknames that you know? Do you think nicknames are positive or negative?

Exploring and Understanding Reading

Our names are an important part of our identity. This reading is about the traditions and practices of giving people names.

PREVIEWING

Preview the reading. List three ideas you think you will learn from this reading.

> ■ *READING TIP: One way to preview is to read the beginning sentence of each paragraph. The first sentence often expresses the main idea of the paragraph.*

1. _____

2. _____

3. _____

Compare your ideas with a partner. Then, read the selection and check your predictions. Remove any ideas that you didn't find. Add any new ideas you found.

The Roots of Our Names

A. Our first name is very familiar and important to us. Someone once estimated that we answer to our name 328,725 times during our lives. For most of us, our first name is given to us by our parents. There are many reasons why people choose to give certain names to their children. One of the most common practices is to name the child after a relative, or after themselves. Other reasons are more individual, like giving a name that has a pleasant sound or a positive association: for example, the name of a flower (Rose, Lily), or a quality (Faith, Joy, Hope). Some names come from famous people in history, like Joan after Joan of Arc or Winston after Winston Churchill. Other names come from famous entertainment personalities, like Elvis after Elvis Presley. Some people give their children names that are popular on television, like Ashley, Holly, or Kelly for girls and Brent, Keith, or Harrison for boys. Some people decide their children's names quickly; others think about the choices for much longer. Sometimes parents buy special baby-naming books and do other research to find the right name for their child.

B. Our names can affect our personal lives. Some studies have found that children with the most popular first names are more favored by others. Some studies in England showed that, on average, children with common names like Mary and David received better grades from their teachers. In all languages there are names that are traditionally given to girls and others that are given to boys. But in English there are some names, like Leslie and Robin, that can be used for either sex. In many languages there is a female and male version of the same name, like Robert for a boy and Roberta for a girl. In many countries people give children a nickname that often is a short form of their first name, like Kate for Kathryn or Mike for Michael. Sometimes our names or nicknames can cause problems. Children who have a name commonly given to the opposite sex, who have an unpopular, old-fashioned, or strange-sounding name or an unusual nickname might be teased or made fun of by others. Sometimes people decide to change their name. They choose a new name to make their lives easier or to be more successful in their careers. Actors like John Wayne and performers like Madonna use stage names. Writers use pen names, or pseudonyms, when they publish their work.

C. Family names also reflect different traditions. In China, people use their family name first and their given name second. In many Spanish-speaking countries, children take the family name of both parents. In Denmark, there are 85,000 different family names, but two-thirds of the population use only 50 of those for their last name. This creates problems for the government. It has trouble keeping files for so many people with the same first and family names. Over the last four hundred years, the Danish government has tried to get people to use different family names but with little success. Some family name changes do occur. When people emigrate to another country, they might change or shorten their family name to fit in better with the general population.

GETTING THE MAIN IDEA

Read the list of main ideas. Write the main idea for each of the paragraphs on the correct line.

MAIN IDEAS

The traditions of family names in different countries.
Some traditions in choosing first names.
The effects that names have on people's lives.

Paragraph A _____

_____

Paragraph B _____

_____

Paragraph C _____

_____

SCANNING: GETTING THE FACTS

■ *READING TIP:* Finding the main ideas helps you to scan for the answers to questions more effectively. When you read one of the questions below, ask yourself, "Which paragraph has the information I need to answer this question?" Then scan that paragraph first.

Answer the following questions. Underline the words in the reading that support your answer.

1. What are some of the traditions for choosing a first name?

   a. _____

   b. _____

   c. _____

2. a. What can happen to children who have a popular name?

   _____

   b. What can happen to children who have an unpopular name?

   _____

3. Why do some people change their names?

   a. _____

   b. _____

4. What are the traditions about family names in

   China: _____

   _____

   Spanish-speaking countries: _____

   _____

   Denmark: _____

   _____

Compare answers with a partner.

NOTE-TAKING

Scan the reading to find information about different traditions or customs in giving people first names and family names. Make a list of four ideas about different traditions or customs in note form.

Traditions/Customs:
First Names

Traditions/Customs:
Family Names

1. _____   _____

   _____   _____

2. _____   _____

   _____   _____

3. _____   _____

   _____   _____

4. _____   _____

   _____   _____

Work with a partner. Take turns explaining the traditions about first and family names to each other.

After Reading

EVALUATING THE INFORMATION: GIVING YOUR OPINION

Step 1. *Individual work*: Think about the following question. Should countries have rules and regulations about the names people can and cannot choose? If yes, what should these rules be? If no, why not?

Step 2. Read the following paragraph. Find and underline facts that show names that are not allowed in different countries.

Step 3. *Pair work:* Compare the information you underlined with a partner. Check to see that you underlined the same information. Discuss your opinions on the questions in Step 1.

■ ■   *New Names: Who Decides?*   ■ ■

Some countries have rules and regulations about the names people can and cannot choose. In France, officials can refuse to register a child's name if they think it is silly, insulting, or vulgar. In Quebec, Canada, there are also rules to follow in choosing a name. One Quebec couple had to fight to keep the name, Tomás, they wanted to give their son. The name was refused because it is written with an accent over the letter *a*. Officials said the accented *a* would make the name difficult for most people to pronounce. But, when the parents insisted that this name reflected their cultural heritage, the officials changed their decision. Another country that has name regulations is Norway. In Norway, a man who wanted to change his name to Harley Davidson, after his motorcycle, was refused. Officials said that Davidson was not a Norwegian name. Another rule is that Norwegians cannot choose a name that might be a social disadvantage for their child. Using the name of a cartoon character or a dictator is not allowed. On the other hand, in some countries, like the United States and England, people may choose any name they wish. In these countries, people can easily change their name by going to court. For a small amount of money, they can legally register their new name.

Step 4. *Group work*: Think about these questions. Share your ideas with others. Choose a group member to make a report of the ideas you discussed and decided on.

a. What are some reasons why a country would refuse to allow a name?

b. What are the advantages (good points) of having rules for names?

c. What are the disadvantages (negative points)?

d. Do you think it is better to have rules or to allow people to choose any name they want?

Vocabulary Building

VOCABULARY IN CONTEXT

Complete each sentence with one of the following words from the reading. Circle the words that helped you decide on your answer.

a. famous   d. popular   f. successful
b. individual   e. silly   g. unusual
c. pleasant

1. She chose a very _____ name that everyone liked.

2. They named their first child Elvis, after the _____ rock 'n' roll singer.

3. She decided to choose a name that had a _____ sound that was easy to pronounce.

4. He bought the picture because it had an _____ look that he had never seen before.

5. It was an _____ choice that only he could make.

6. She changed her name to be more _____ in her career.

7. She was afraid that her name would sound _____ to other people.

Check your answers. Work with a partner and take turns reading the completed sentences.

SYNONYMS

Circle the word that is closest in meaning to the word in boldface.

1. **allow**   leave   lift   let   lower

2. **choose**   select   suspend   separate   supply

3. **change**   advance   advise   alter   advantage

4. **create**   move   motivate   motion   make

5. **decide**   chance   choose   change   close

6. **receive**   give   get   go   grow

7. **refuse**   return   reject   reflect   remain

8. **register**   record   reason   repeat   read

Write three sentences using words from the list.

a. _____

b. _____

c. _____

Expanding Your Language

SPEAKING

Oral Presentation: What are some customs for choosing names in your family or in your culture? Prepare information for a short (two-minute) talk on this subject. To help you get started, ask others in your class what they would like to know about the customs of choosing names. Think about the content of your talk. Try to give a few interesting details for each idea you explain. Put your ideas in order. Write your ideas in note form. Practice once or twice so that you are comfortable explaining the information to others. Present your information to a partner or in a small group.

WRITING

Topic Writing: From the ideas you have gathered in this chapter and your own experience, write about some customs of choosing names that are important or interesting to you. Follow the instructions for Topic Writing in Chapter 1, page 13.

Opinion Writing: Write about whether or not countries should make rules about the names people can choose for themselves or their children. Use information from the reading to support your ideas. Include any ideas or examples of your own.

CHAPTER 5

Researching Our Hidden Roots

Chapter Openers

LISTING IDEAS

What special or surprising events could lead you to look into your family history? Give some reasons that people could have for finding out about their family history.

1. inheriting money from an unknown relative

2. _____

3. _____

4. _____

Share your ideas with a partner or with a small group.

CATEGORIZING

Check (✔) the category you think best fits each of these feelings.

Feelings	Positive	Negative	Neutral (Either/Both)
lonely	_____	_____	_____
stunned	_____	_____	_____
amazed	_____	_____	_____
excited	_____	_____	_____
nervous	_____	_____	_____
embarrassed	_____	_____	_____
uncomfortable	_____	_____	_____
angry	_____	_____	_____
thrilled	_____	_____	_____
surprised	_____	_____	_____
overjoyed	_____	_____	_____
curious	_____	_____	_____
upset	_____	_____	_____

Compare answers with a partner. Choose several of these feelings and talk about times when you felt that way.

Choose one of the readings. Work with a partner who is reading the same story.

■ ■

Reading 1: John's Story

Read this selection quickly and answer the following question:

What surprising information did John find out?

_____

_____

A. John O'Neill was an only child who lived with his parents in Albany, New York. The O'Neills had a lot of friends but not many relatives. John knew his mother had a half sister who lived in California, but John had never met her. John's mother didn't have much contact with her sister. John's father was an only child, just like his son. When John was twenty years old, his parents died in a car accident and John was left alone in the large house where he had grown up. John felt lonely and uncomfortable living in his childhood home, so he decided to sell the house. Once the house was sold, he had to look through all the papers and the belongings of his parents and decide what memorabilia he wanted to keep to remember them by and what to throw away.

B.   One afternoon John found a large, thick envelope filled with official-looking papers and some twenty-year-old newspaper clippings. He started to read and was amazed by what he learned. According to the papers, he had been adopted by his parents when he was an infant. Even more curious was the fact that another child, a girl, had been born at the same time. He had a twin sister somewhere. John was stunned. He felt angry that his parents hadn't told him about his background but thrilled to think that he might have family he had not known about. Now he had to try to find the sister he had no memories of. He wondered where his investigation would take him. To begin with, he had the name of the hospital where he and his sister were born. He decided to start his search there.

INFORMATION QUESTIONS

Look for the answers to these questions. Underline the words in the story that support your answer.

1. What was the size of John's family?

   _____

   _____

2. What did John find after his parents died?

   _____

   _____

3. What two things did John find out about his background?

   a. _____

   b. _____

4. a. What did John decide to do?

   _____

   b. How was he going to begin?

   _____

Work with a partner. Try to agree on the same answers. Refer to the reading in cases where you disagree.

NOTE-TAKING

List the facts of the story in note form on pages of your own.

John's story
- an only child

_____

_____

_____

RECAPPING THE STORY

Work with a partner who took notes on the same story.

1. Orally, compare the list of facts you wrote.
2. Check that the facts you wrote are clear and understandable.
3. Refer to the reading if you have different information.
4. Change or add to the facts you noted as necessary.
5. Take turns to practice reporting the information.

REACTING TO THE STORY

Share your ideas about these questions with a partner.

1. If you were John, how would you feel?
2. What questions would John want to ask his sister?
3. How do you think this story could end?

Reading 2: Joy's Story

Read this selection quickly and answer the following question:

What surprising information did Joy find out?

_____

_____

A.   Joy Kaplan was newly married and had just moved from Chicago to San Francisco with her husband. Soon after moving she found that she was pregnant. She was overjoyed at the idea of having a baby but a little worried about being far from her family, her friends, and all the support she had back home. She asked several people for recommendations, chose a doctor near her home, and made an initial appointment. Because she was a new patient, the doctor asked her a lot of questions about her family. He asked about the ages and medical history of her brothers and sisters, her parents, her aunts and uncles, and even her grandparents. Joy was surprised to find that she didn't have a lot of answers for the doctor. She felt uncomfortable and embarrassed about the amount of information she didn't have. Why did the doctor need information such as her grandparents' medical history? The doctor understood her feelings and wasn't surprised at her reaction.

B.   The doctor knew Joy was upset, so he explained that he had important, life-saving reasons for finding out about the medical histories of her relatives. This information could help her have a healthy pregnancy. If there was a family history of diabetes or heart disease, the doctor would watch for signs of these problems during Joy's pregnancy. Also, he could help identify medical problems the unborn baby might have and, if possible, prevent or prepare to treat them. The doctor needed to know if there had been any genetically transmitted diseases in her or her husband's family. He wanted to know if her mother had had problems such as miscarriages or premature births in her pregnancies. He also wanted to know if there was a family history of multiple births, such as twins or triplets. Joy thought she remembered that one of her grandmothers had a twin brother or sister, and she was curious. Did this mean that there was a greater chance that she could have twins? Were there any hidden medical problems she didn't know about? Where should she begin to look? The doctor suggested she start her medical history by asking her parents for information about as many of her relatives as possible. Joy was excited but a little nervous about what she might discover. She decided to begin by phoning her parents and her parents-in-law that evening.

_____

INFORMATION QUESTIONS

Look for the answers to these questions. Underline the words in the story that support your answer.

1. Why did Joy move to a new city?

    _____

    _____

2. How did Joy feel about her pregnancy?

    _____

    _____

3. a. What questions did the doctor ask her?

    _____

    _____

    b. How did she feel about the doctor's questions?

    _____

    _____

4. What two reasons did the doctor give Joy for the questions he asked?

   a. _____

   b. _____

5. What are some examples of medical conditions the doctor wanted to know about?

   a. _____

   b. _____

   c. _____

6. What did Joy decide to do?

   _____

Work with a partner. Try to agree on the answers. Refer to the reading in cases where you disagree.

NOTE-TAKING

List the facts of the story in note form on pages of your own.

Joy's story
- newly married

_____

_____

_____

RECAPPING THE STORY

Work with a partner who took notes about the same story. Follow the instructions for recapping on page 56.

REACTING TO THE STORY

Share your ideas about these questions with a partner.

1. If you were Joy, how would you feel?
2. What questions do you think Joy should ask her family?
3. How do you think this story could end?

After Reading

RETELLING THE STORY

Work with a partner who took notes about the other story. Use your notes to retell the information.

COMPARING THE STORIES

Answer these questions based on the information from the stories.

1. What is each person's motivation for finding out about his or her past?
2. What are the similarities and differences in the two stories?
3. What do you think could be the conclusion of these stories? What do you think John and Joy will find out? How could they discover this information?

Vocabulary Building

VOCABULARY IN CONTEXT

Use your understanding of one part of the sentence to help you guess the verb/preposition combination that is missing. Remember that sometimes when a verb is followed by a preposition, it has a special meaning.

Complete each sentence with one of the following word phrases.

a. adopted by   d. look through   f. watch for

b. grown up   e. throw away   g. worried about

c. known about

1. He decided to _____ all the papers he found to try to locate the name he needed.

2. He didn't know that he had been _____ his parents when he was a baby.

3. She wondered why she hadn't _____ her mother's first marriage.

4. She had _____ in a small family and liked to visit them often.

5. She had too many papers to keep, so she decided to

   _____ half of them.

6. Joy didn't want to be _____ the pregnancy, but she was.

7. He told her what signs of trouble she should

   _____.

Check your answers. Work with a partner and take turns reading your sentences.

WORD FORMS

Choose the correct word to complete the sentences. Use your knowledge of grammar rules, i.e., if the word is a noun, adjective, verb, or adverb, to help you choose.

1. pregnant / pregnancy

   a. She was very happy when she found out about her

      _____.

   b. She told the doctor that she thought she was

      _____.

2. genetic / genetically

   a. She was worried that she could have inherited a

      _____ disease.

   b. She was worried that the disease could be transmitted

      _____.

3. question / questioned

   a. She decided she would ask her doctor the _____ that was on her mind.

   b. She wondered about the doctor's decision and

      _____ him about it.

4. memories / remember / memorabilia

    a. He looked through all the _____ to see what he wanted to keep.

    b. She tried to _____ her grandmother's medical history.

    c. She had a lot of _____ of her grandmother, but nothing was written down.

Expanding Your Language

WRITING

Reacting to a Story: Use your notes to write about one of the stories. Write your own reaction to the story. What do you think the person should do?

SPEAKING

Role-play: Work with a partner. Choose one of the stories to act out. Write out a conversation based on the ideas in the story. You may want to add characters (such as a friend for John to talk to or Joy's husband) to the story. Here is one example of how to begin the conversation:

John: Can you meet me at the cafe? The most amazing thing just happened. I have to talk to you.

Friend: Sure. I can be at the cafe in ten minutes.

Use your lines to act out the story, but do not memorize the lines. Be creative.

CHAPTER 6

Writing Our Own History

Chapter Openers

PERSONALIZING

■ READING TIP:
Thinking about your own ideas and experiences on a topic is called personalizing. This helps you to recognize language in the reading and will help you understand more easily.

Imagine that your grandmother gave you a scrapbook about her life. What do you think the scrapbook would contain? List as many ideas as you can.

1. her wedding invitation

2. _____

3. _____

4. _____

CHECKLIST

Check the ways that you record important events in your life or in the life of your family.

_____ Photographs

_____ Videotape

_____ Letters to family or friends

_____ Journal writing

_____ Audiotape

_____ Memorabilia (for example, ticket stubs, program notes, etc.)

Other: _____

Work with a partner. Choose two important events in your life. Describe what you remember about what happened. Tell how you recorded these events.

▋ Exploring and Understanding Reading

This reading explains one woman's ideas on the importance of writing autobiographies.

PREVIEWING

Look at the title and subtitle. What do you predict the reading will be about?

1. _____

2. _____

3. _____

SKIMMING

Skim the reading and see if your predictions were correct. If you think you were wrong, change your prediction. After your quick reading, answer these general questions.

■ *READING TIP:*
Skimming is a useful strategy when you have a longer reading with difficult or unfamiliar vocabulary. When you skim, you skip over the words you don't know and focus on what you can understand. Read for the general idea.

1. What does Marie Bolton think it is important to do?

   _____

   _____

2. Why does she think it's important?

   _____

   _____

Autobiographical writing helps us record memories, feel connected

Our Own Stories

By ANN DOUGLAS, *Chicago Tribune*

PETERBOROUGH, Ont.—One of Marie Bolton's greatest treasures is a scrapbook that was lovingly compiled for her by her grandmother. It's filled with photos, postcards, poems, Christmas cards, and other memorabilia accumulated over the course of ninety-four years.

Bolton sees the scrapbook as a precious legacy from her grandmother, who is no longer living.

"When I read the scrapbook, I learn things about my grandmother that I wouldn't otherwise have known," Bolton explained. "I discover her feelings about the grandfather I never knew. I hear her recall the joy and wonder of caring for her babies when they were young, and I witness world events like the end of World War I as seen through her eyes."

Bolton, 33, a freelance writer in Peterborough, was so moved by the scrapbook that she began leading workshops on the art of memoir writing.

"It's my way of encouraging others, particularly older people, to write about their lives. Many people are reluctant to write about themselves because they feel that their life has been terribly ordinary and is not likely to be of interest to anyone else.

"I believe that we all have a story to tell, and that we owe it to others to share our experience."

Autobiographical writing doesn't have to be that difficult, Bolton said.

"It's important to give yourself permission to start and stop the project as your time and interest permit," she said.

"Sometimes it's necessary to put the project aside for a few weeks or even months if things get particularly busy at home or at work."

Bolton said the hardest part of autobiographical writing is getting started.

"If you're lucky enough to have a closet full of shoeboxes filled with treasures that date back years and years, flip through these boxes and start to think about how the various pieces fit into the major periods in your life, i.e., childhood, school days, career, marriage, childbearing, retirement, etc.

"Then purchase a scrapbook and start piecing your materials together chronologically. Select photos, artwork, report cards, ticket stubs, wedding invitations, and other memorabilia that are significant to you, and then record the memories that they trigger for you."

Judy Brenna, 55, took this type of approach when she sat down to record her family memories.

"Last Christmas, I put together a binder of all my family's recipes for my four children. With each recipe, I included a paragraph about how I came by the recipe and whose recipe it was.

"It turned into a trip down memory lane, remembering when I was a child helping my mother to duplicate her mother's favorite family dishes or when I was a young bride trying to re-create my husband's mother's perfect recipe.

"I ended up creating something of a family history of happy times spent in the kitchen and around the dining room table."

While creating a scrapbook can be time-consuming, it's probably one of the most important projects you'll ever undertake, Bolton said.

"My grandmother has been dead for two years now," she said. "While I can no longer chat with her over a cup of tea about days gone by, I can flip through the scrapbook and reflect on her memories of yesteryear.

"It helps me to remember her and to get an appreciation of what it's like to live a long and happy life. That's her legacy to me."

CHECKING THE FACTS

A. Circle T for true and F for false. Underline the information in the reading that supports your answer.

1. T   F   Marie Bolton's grandmother is still living.

2. T   F   Marie decided to teach others to write memoirs.

3. T   F   People feel that their lives are interesting to many others.

4. T   F   The easiest part of writing autobiographies is getting started.

5. T   F   Marie likes to look through her grandmother's scrapbook.

B. Search the reading to answer the following questions.

1. What are three things that Marie learned about her grand-mother?

  a. _____

  b. _____

  c. _____

2. What work does Marie Bolton do?

  _____

3. What are six major periods of a person's life?

  a. _____   d. _____

  b. _____   e. _____

  c. _____   f. _____

4. What are the steps for creating a scrapbook?

  a. Start collecting and organizing memorabilia.

  b. Purchase _____

  c. Start _____

  d. Select _____

  e. Record _____

5. What are two reasons why Marie feels creating a scrapbook is important?

  a. _____

  b. _____

Work with a partner. Take turns reading the questions and answers orally. Refer to the reading in cases where you disagree.

RELATING MAIN IDEAS AND DETAILS

Reread the story quickly and underline the details for each of the following main ideas. Write the letter of each main idea in the margin where you found the details.

A. The gift Marie Bolton got.

B. The work Marie Bolton does.

C. The steps to creating a scrapbook.

D. The importance of Marie Bolton's work.

Work with a partner. Take turns explaining the details of these ideas in your own words.

After Reading

GIVING YOUR OPINION

Decide if you agree or disagree with these statements taken from the reading. Be prepared to explain the reasons for your opinions.

1. Many people feel that their life has been terribly ordinary and is not likely to be of interest to anyone else.
2. I believe that we all have a story to tell, and that we owe it to others to share our experience.

Share your ideas with a partner or with a small group. Together find another statement from the reading that you think is interesting or important. Discuss the reasons for your choice.

APPLYING THE INFORMATION: DISCOVERING THE REASONS PEOPLE WRITE

In the first reading Marie Bolton lists some reasons people write about their own lives. These reasons include the following:

A. Recording our thoughts and feelings about things that happened.

B. Witnessing world events in a personal way.

C. Feeling connected to others.

D. Finding out about important life events.

E. Recording memories for the future.

The following is a short autobiographical story. Read the story and, as you read, think about the list of reasons from the first reading in the unit. What do you think the author's reason is for writing? Circle the reason(s) in the list on page 69.

■ ■
────────────

My Life as a Sandwich

By DR. BARBARA ROBACK

A. There were three of them, aged 87, 89, and 91, all sisters of my mother. They are in varying states of decline now—one in a foster home, one in a chronic care facility, and the eldest one still living alone, despite the lack of vision, hearing, balance, and judgment. She, of course, insists that she's fine and continues to smoke, fall, and give money away to the drug-store delivery man. He is doing nicely, thank you, with his secondhand stretch limo, thanks to quite a few of those "loans." Meanwhile, various agency workers and one niece tear out their increasingly gray hair. She has recently started having hallucinations about Greek and Roman statues. "Is that frightening?" I ask. "No, I saw statues as a child when I was in Europe," she says matter-of-factly.

B. On the other jaw of the vice grip are my six-year-old boys, fraternal twins, who need endless cuddling, stories, baths, lunches, lifts to lessons, nagging, and refereeing. They don't understand why they have to visit smelly institutions where old people scream and try to hug them. Nor do they understand why their mother yells at her 91-year-old aunt for giving thousands of dollars away. Such is the life of my generation, sandwiched as we are between caring for aging relatives and young children. Most of us, out of desire and necessity, also work outside the home. Where is the time or energy for keeping the marriage fires burning?

C. But there are significant rewards that come from life in a vice. This summer I packed up one aunt's abandoned apartment. She had been an invalid most of her life; teenage tuberculosis had robbed her of her strength and mobility. Because I lost both my parents at a young age, she became guardian to me and my older sister, doing the best she could to care for both of us. As a teenager I was embarrassed by my abnormal family and retreated into writing stories about imaginary characters who led truly wonderful lives. But this summer, as I sifted through the remains of years of accumulation I found some amazing treasures: my mother's

high school ring from 1936, my sister's hospital birth tag, a desperate letter written by my mother, overwhelmed with the responsibility of caring
for her dying husband and her two too young daughters. And then, the
ceremonial wine from my parents' wedding, lovingly kept from 1939. My
years of shame and resentment evaporated. I was now back to myself.

D.   My aunt was a superb seamstress and her fabrics, sewing machine, and
     threads have been donated to help equip a Training Center for immigrant
     women to become employable. My aunt is settled in her new hospital
     home. I beg and bribe my children into visiting her with promises of
     treats. They walk down the hallway holding their noses. But in the end,
     they do kiss her good-bye. And I pray they are learning something impor-
     tant about human decency.

Vocabulary Building

VOCABULARY IN CONTEXT

**You can understand the meaning of a new word by using the
words you know to help you make a good guess. Circle the words
that help you to guess the meaning of words in boldface.**

1. In this unit you will read about one of the fastest-growing interests in North America—**genealogy**. Looking into our family history is the third most popular hobby in the United States.
2. It's filled with different items from the past, like photos, postcards, poems, Christmas cards, and other **memorabilia** accumulated over the course of ninety-four years.
3. I **witness** events like the end of World War I as seen through
   her eyes.
4. Many people are **reluctant** to write about themselves. They hesi-
   tate because they feel that their life has been terribly ordinary
   and is not likely to be of interest to anyone else.
5. Start to think about how the various pieces fit into the major
   periods of your life, i.e., childhood, school days, career, marriage,
   retirement, etc. Then, purchase a scrapbook and start piecing
   your materials together **chronologically**.
6. My grandmother has been dead for two years now. But the scrapbook she made helps me to remember her and to get an appreciation of what it's like to live a long and happy life. That's her
   legacy to me.

WORD FORMS: ROOTS

Words that come from the same root, like these words from the Latin *memorabilis*, have similar meanings. Choose the correct word to complete the sentence.

memoir / remember / memorabilia / memories

1. I have a lot of very warm _____ of growing up in my grandmother's house.

2. I gathered all the _____ my mother had collected and put them into a big box.

3. I tried to create a book that would help people _____ this special time in their lives.

4. She decided to begin to write a _____ of her own life.

MATCHING MEANINGS

Match the phrases in Column A to those closest in meaning in Column B.

Column A

_____ 1. end up

_____ 2. put together

_____ 3. flip through

_____ 4. chat with

_____ 5. be moved by

_____ 6. reflect on

Column B

a. look at something quickly

b. have strong feelings

c. talk about everyday events

d. have a final product

e. create something from different parts

f. think about the meaning of things

Expanding Your Language

SPEAKING

A. Tell and Retell: Quickly reread the story "My Life as a Sandwich." Highlight the important details of the story. Get together with a partner. Take turns telling the information in each paragraph. Tell as much as you can remember.

B. Two-Minute Taped Talk: Choose a person who is important to you. It can be a family member, a friend, or someone you admire. Prepare a two-minute audiotape to talk about this person and the effect they have had on your life. Base your talk on your own ideas and the information in this chapter. Make a short outline of your ideas in note form. Practice your talk a few times before you record.

WRITING

Topic Writing: Imagine that you are going to make a scrapbook about your life. Choose three items of memorabilia that you would include and write about what each one means to you. Follow the instructions in Chapter 1, page 13.

Read On: Taking It Further

READING SUGGESTIONS

■ *READING TIP:*
Remember to write your reading journal and add vocabulary log entries to your journal.

Ask your teacher to recommend some easy-to-read autobiography or biography titles for you to choose from. Reading these types of stories is a good way to find out about people and the times and places they lived in.

Sample Suggestion: In *Roots* Alex Haley wrote about his family history, going back to when one of his ancestors was brought from Africa into the United States as a slave. Haley's family story is very interesting. You could find out about this story by looking for the video of the television program based on his book.

Money Matters

When Money Talks, the World Keeps Silent
—SWEDISH PROVERB

Introducing the Topics

Money affects our daily lives. It influences the way we feel, think, and act. This unit will look into some interesting questions about money. Chapter 7 will examine what young people can learn about the value of money. Is a person ever too young to start thinking about budgets and savings? Chapter 8 looks at the impact of lotteries on people's lives. Lotteries and other forms of gambling are popular in many countries. Are they a good thing? Chapter 9 is about the future of money. Will credit, debit, and other bank cards totally replace cash? How will this affect our attitudes toward money?

Points of Interest

EXPRESSIONS

Read and decide if you think each expression shows a positive, negative, or neutral attitude toward money. Check (✔) the category you decide on.

	Positive	Negative	Neutral
1. Love of money is the root of all evil.	_____	_____	_____
2. A penny saved is a penny earned.	_____	_____	_____
3. Time is money.	_____	_____	_____
4. Money can't buy love.	_____	_____	_____
5. Money doesn't grow on trees.	_____	_____	_____
6. Money speaks in a language all nations understand.	_____	_____	_____

Work with a partner. Discuss what the expressions mean and try to agree on the best category for each.

CHAPTER 7

Starting Young: Learning the Value of Money

Chapter Openers

DISCUSSION QUESTIONS

Think about these questions. Share your ideas with a partner or with a small group.

1. Have you ever made budget and savings plans for yourself?

2. What are some common problems that people have when they try to save and budget money?

3. a. Did you ever get an allowance (money from your parents)?
   b. What was it for?

4. How much allowance money should a child have at the following ages: 2–5, 6–11, 12–16, 16–18?

5. Who taught you the most about handling money?
   a. Mother
   b. Father
   c. Both mother and father
   d. Teacher
   e. Friend or other

Exploring and Understanding Reading

PREDICTING

Circle A if you agree or D if you disagree with the statement.

1. A   D   Children usually know how much money their parents make.

2. A   D   It is a good idea to give children an allowance at age two.

3. A   D   Children learn about money from their parents' example.

4. A   D   At age seven, children can learn to shop for the best price.

5. A   D   Children should start saving for college by age twelve.

6. A   D   Teenagers should not work after school.

Work with a partner. Compare your answers. You don't have to agree, but explain your reasons as completely as possible. After you finish reading, return to these questions and answer them based on the information you read.

SKIMMING

Read the selection quickly and choose the statement that best expresses the general idea of the reading as a whole.

A. Parents should not talk about money with their children until they are older.

B. Parents should get experts to teach their children about money.

C. Parents should give their children different advice about money depending on their age.

Can We Teach Kids to Save?

A. Money management experts think that children need to learn about money at an early age. They advise parents to give kids four years old or younger, a weekly allowance. Experts suggest parents give preschool children two or three dollars a week and then add a dollar at every birthday. This might seem like a large amount of money for a child that young. However, experts say that if parents want their children to understand how to budget money, it's not. Even preschool children can learn the value of money.

B. Young children don't always know how much money their parents make, or understand how their parent's earnings affect them. But parents can help their children develop some very important attitudes no matter what their incomes are. Kids can learn to tell the difference between what they want and what they need. They can learn how to make a budget and how to keep spending within that budget. For example, when children want an expensive toy that costs more than they have in allowance, parents can help them to figure out how many weeks it will take to save the money to buy it. In the end, the most important way parents influence their children's attitude toward money is by setting a good example of responsible money management in the way they budget, spend, and save money themselves.

C. Here are some age-specific suggestions for teaching responsible attitudes toward money.

AGES 2–5

- Give a small allowance ($2–3) each week. It can be for doing chores (making their bed, tidying their clothes, etc.) or not.

- Let children pay for some of the things they want, like a toy or a special treat.

- Budget a certain amount of the money for savings.

- Discuss what they will use their savings for, i.e., school, travel, gifts, etc.

AGES 6–12

- Increase their allowance gradually to match their age ($6 or 7 for a six-year-old). Show children how to make a budget.

- Set up a savings account at the bank in the child's name.

- Talk about ways to earn extra money (doing special chores and small jobs in the neighborhood like shoveling snow or raking leaves).

- Show children how to be better consumers by shopping for the best price.

AGES 13–17

- Encourage children to earn more money of their own at small jobs after school.

- Give children responsibility for paying part of their school or extracurricular expenses like sports equipment or musical instruments.

- Have children open a checking account and handle their own money.

- Have children save money for future schooling costs such as college tuition.

If kids start on the road to good money management when they are young, they will be learning an important life skill. They may make some mistakes along the way, but they will learn the basics of saving, investing, budgeting, and wise spending. Kids who learn about money early are often good at making money later. And that's good news for parents.

UNDERSTANDING DETAILS

Circle the correct answer. Underline the words in the reading that support your answer.

1. Experts suggest that parents begin to give children an allowance

   at age _____.
   a. two or three
   b. six or seven
   c. eight or nine

2. Children often _____ how much money their parents earn.
   a. know
   b. don't know

3. Children _____ learn the difference between what they want and what they need.
   a. can
   b. can't

4. Parents can influence their children's attitude toward money the

   most by _____.
   a. telling them what to do
   b. setting a good example

5. Children can start to work after school at age _____.
   a. seven
   b. ten
   c. fourteen

6. It's good for kids to learn money management at a young age

   because they will _____.
   a. learn to spend wisely
   b. spend more money
   c. make more money later

Compare answers with a partner. Look back at the reading if you disagree.

REACTING TO THE STORY

Share your ideas about these questions with a partner or a small group.

1. a. Is it possible for parents to teach their children positive attitudes toward money?

   b. How difficult or how easy is it? How important is it?

2. When do we learn our attitudes toward money? Can these attitudes change?

After Reading

APPLYING THE INFORMATION: PROBLEM SOLVING

Based on the information you read, what would you suggest in the following situations?

1. Your seventeen-year-old wants to apply for a university that has a very high tuition.

   Suggestions: _____

   _____

2. You are out shopping and your five-year-old asks you to buy an expensive toy that is being advertised on TV.

   Suggestions: _____

   _____

3. Your fourteen-year-old wants to get a part-time job after school.

   Suggestions: _____

   _____

4. Your eleven-year-old wants to do extra chores to earn more money.

   Suggestions: _____

   _____

Compare your suggestions. Make a list of the best suggestions and report them to your class.

EVALUATING THE INFORMATION

Read the short article that follows and then discuss these questions.

1. What is this child doing?
2. What is this child and the children he advises learning?
3. What are the positive points of this boy's job? What information surprises you?
4. Should this child be working? Why, or why not?

Should This Child Be Working?

Andrew Burns, all of nine years old, greets customers in his capacity as president of the Children's Bank at Enterprise Bank of Omaha. "I understand banking," says the fourth-grader, who dreamed up the job and then applied for it at his father's bank. "And I'm a kid. I know what their needs are." Among the kiddy bank's services are making loans of up to $100 to youngsters (with an adult cosigner) and letting paper carriers and other kids with jobs deposit money in zipper bags the way businesses do. There's also a teller window low enough for children to reach. Andrew comes in two or three times a week to serve his clientele. "If they're in trouble with money, if they need some advice, I help them," he says.

There are many approaches to the subject of money. These can differ from family to family and from country to country. From your own experience, give your opinion of some of the suggestions in the reading. Discuss one or more of these questions with a partner or with a small group.

1. Should teenagers work to make money while still in school?
2. Should children know details of the family budget?
3. Should young people borrow money to complete their college education?

Vocabulary Building

VOCABULARY IN CONTEXT

Complete each sentence with one of the following phrases. Use your understanding of the general meaning of the sentence to help you.

a. tell the difference

b. make a budget

c. keep their spending

d. figure out

e. setting a good example

1. Kids can learn to _____ between what they want and what they need.

2. Parents influence their children's attitude toward money by

_____ of responsible money management.

3. Kids can learn how to _____ and save even at a young age.

4. Parents can help kids _____ how long it will take to save the money to buy what they want.

5. Kids can learn how to _____ within their budget.

Check your answers. Work with a partner and take turns reading your sentences.

GIVING MORE ADVICE: SENTENCE FORM

Find five sentences that start with verbs and that give advice.

Example: <u>Save</u> money for future schooling costs such as college tuition.
    Verb

Write the sentence. Underline the verb.

1. _____

2. _____

3. _____

4. _____

5. _____

Work with a partner and take turns reading your sentences. Give the meaning of the words you underlined.

Expanding Your Language

SPEAKING: ORAL PRESENTATIONS

1. Bring money from your country or another country of your choice. Prepare to talk about this currency to others in a small group. Present some interesting facts. For example, discuss different types of currency and their value, or describe any pictures or writing shown on the bills. Compare information with those who brought money from other countries.

QUESTIONNAIRE

Answer these questions. Think about the reasons for your answers. Then interview two people and write their answers.

	Your answers	*Person A*	*Person B*
1.	_____	_____	_____
2.	_____	_____	_____
3.	_____	_____	_____
4.	_____	_____	_____

1. How would you describe your attitude toward money?
   a. I'm a spender.   c. I don't like to think about money.
   b. I'm a saver.   d. I'm worried I won't have enough.

2. How much do you think our personalities influence our attitude toward money?
   a. Personality has a strong influence.
   b. Personality has some influence.
   c. Personality has little influence.
   d. Personality has no influence.

3. When did your present attitude toward money develop the most?
   a. Childhood   c. Adulthood   e. Old age
   b. Adolescence   d. Middle age

4. How do people's needs for money change in the different periods of their life?
   a. Adolescence   c. Middle age
   b. Adulthood   d. Old age

Writing

Choose one of the topics or a topic of your own. Write as much as you can about your topic.

1. What are your ideas about the importance of money in society? How does your attitude compare with that of others you know?

2. At what age do you think young people should be allowed to work?

Follow the writing instructions in Chapter 1 on page 12.

CHAPTER 8

Lotteries—Good for Society?

Chapter Openers

IN-CLASS SURVEY

Circle the answer you agree with. Interview two others in your class. Find out their opinion.

1. Why do people decide to buy lottery tickets?

2. What do you think the chances are of winning a lottery?
   a. Small.   b. Very small.

3. Do the lives of lottery winners change?
   a. Yes, in a positive way.   b. Yes, in a negative way.
   c. No, they do not change at all.

4. Should lotteries be advertised on television? Why or why not?

5. Have you ever bought a lottery ticket?
   a. Yes.   b. No.   c. Sometimes.

Discuss your answers with a partner or with a small group. Share the information with the class.

GETTING INFORMATION FROM A GRAPH

Read the information from the graph to answer these questions.

1. Why do most people decide to buy a lottery ticket?
2. How do the results of this graph compare with the ideas you found out about from the survey?

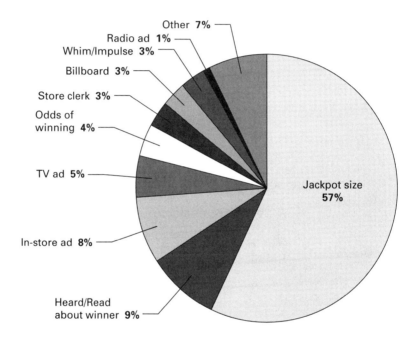

PERSONALIZING

These are two very different stories about the experiences of people who have bought lottery tickets. Before choosing your story, think about the positive and negative ways playing the lottery might affect you.

List three positive or negative points of playing the lottery.

	Positive	*Negative*
1.	_____	_____
	_____	_____
2.	_____	_____
	_____	_____
3.	_____	_____
	_____	_____

Discuss your ideas with a partner.

PAIRED READINGS

Choose one of the readings. Work with a partner who is reading the same information.

SKIMMING

Read your story and answer this question: Did the lottery players(s) in this story have a positive or a negative experience? Explain.

Positive: _____

Negative: _____

Compare answers with a partner. Explain the reasons for your answer.

SCANNING

Look for the answers to the questions after each paragraph. Underline the words in the paragraph that support the answer.

Reading 1: Against All Odds

A. The town of Roby, Texas, is not a rich one. On average, people earn a little under $20,000 a year, and the population is only about 600. Most of the people are farmers. There aren't many well-paying jobs. In fact, most jobs pay only about minimum wage. The people in the town have had a lot of bad luck. They have experienced drought, and falling prices for cattle. Many of the farmers have had serious financial trouble. Some families were worried that the banks were going to take away their farms. On Thanksgiving weekend in November 1997 many families felt unhappy as they sat down to their turkey dinner. Some thought that it would be the last Thanksgiving in their homes.

1. What two facts show that Roby, Texas, is not a rich town?

a. _____

b. _____

2. What kind of wage do most jobs pay?

_____

3. What two problems have the farmers had?

    a. _____

    b. _____

4. Why were people unhappy at Thanksgiving?

    _____

B.   But over the Thanksgiving weekend a miracle happened. A group of 43 townspeople each won part of a $46.7 million dollar prize in the Texas state lottery. They won because they had all joined a lottery pool by putting in $10 each. They bought 430 tickets. Each person will take home about $40,000, after taxes, for the next twenty years. The winners were very happy and grateful. Twenty-eight of the winners were farmers. They're not planning on taking any expensive vacations or buying luxury homes. They plan to pay off the debts on their farms. One man said that the money will allow him to keep on farming instead of looking for a second job. Another said that he had been days away from giving up and leaving the town forever. The winners say that no one is planning to quit a paying job no matter how little money it brings. "Just now," said one, "I might think about buying a new pickup truck for the farm." But another man said that he and his wife wouldn't buy anything new. They plan to start saving money for college educations for their three children.

1. What miracle happened over the Thanksgiving weekend?

    _____

2. How did people join the lottery pool?

    _____

3. What did people win?

    _____

4. What are two ways that people will use their money?

    a. _____

    b. _____

5. What are two ways that people will not spend their money?

    a. _____

    b. _____

C. In the United States lotteries are big business. There are lotteries in at least thirty-seven states and in the District of Columbia. Americans spend more than $88 million every day in lottery games. In 1990 U.S. lotteries made a profit of $10 billion on sales of $20 billion. That makes lotteries the twenty-fourth largest company in sales in the United States. The lottery winners in Roby, Texas, are happy that they played the lottery. Life will go on as it has for years in Roby, thanks in part to a bit of good lottery luck.

_____

1. Where are there lotteries in the United States?

   _____

2. How much money do Americans spend on lotteries every day?

   _____

3. How much money do lotteries make every year:

   a. in sales?_____

   b. in profit?_____

Compare answers with your partner. Try to agree on the same answer. Refer to the reading in cases where you disagree.

RECAPPING THE STORY

List the facts of the story in note form.

Against all odds
- Life in Roby, Texas
  People earn a little under $20,000/year
  Only about 600 people left in town

   _____

   _____

   _____

   _____

Work with a partner who took notes about the same story. Take turns explaining several of the facts to each other. Check to make sure that you both have the same information. Add any facts you didn't note. Correct any facts you need to.

REACTING TO THE STORY

Share your ideas about these questions with a partner.

1. Did the lottery winners in Roby use their winnings in a positive way?
2. Is the lottery an answer to people's financial problems?
3. Does this story show the positive or the negative side of lotteries?

SCANNING

Look for the answers to the questions after each paragraph. Underline the words in the paragraph that support the answer.

■ ■

Reading 2: Beating the Odds

A. Andy D. (not a real name) was a successful businessman who owned a small restaurant. He was married and had two children. But he had a problem. He loved to gamble. He would spend his vacations and week-ends gambling at the casinos. Since he made over $100,000 a year, he felt he could afford his one bad habit. Then in 1982, Andy bought his first lottery ticket. He liked the idea of winning $1 million for a $1 investment. But, soon, he was spending up to $250 a day on lottery tickets. Andy was out of control. Over an eight-year period he estimated that he lost over $100,000 on lottery tickets. As Andy spent more and more on lottery tick-ets, his business began to fail. Finally, he lost his restaurant and his job and found himself over $1 million in debt. When his wife divorced him, he had to move in with his mother. But, as things got worse, his desire to win the lottery increased. He promised his son that he would get a job and get help. He promised his daughter that he would pay for her col-lege tuition. He made promises but he couldn't stop gambling. Finally, on the day his daughter's tuition bill had to be paid, he stole some money from his mother and spent it trying to win at three different lottery games. He lost all of them. In despair, he tried to commit suicide.

1. Who is Andy D.?

   _____

2. What problem does he have?

   _____

3. How much money did he spend on lottery tickets?

   _____

4. What three problems did Andy's habit cause?

   a. _____

   b. _____

   c. _____

5. What did Andy try to do when he lost three lottery games?

   _____

B. Andy was in a hospital for three weeks. The doctors and nurses helped him to recover from the suicide attempt. They encouraged Andy to join a self-help group, Gamblers Anonymous. With the help of this group, Andy began to change. Through the group, he got the support of professionals who helped him to find a job. He also got financial help. He made a monthly budget so that he could repay his debts. After six years, Andy began to see that he would be able to pay off the money he owed. Most of all, Andy stopped buying lottery tickets. Today, he is able to help pay for his children's university tuition bills. The real reward for Andy is that his children believe in him and respect him. Andy is happy to know that he has won back his children's trust. He is beginning to realize that he can get the peace and happiness he always wanted without having to win a lottery.

1. How long was Andy in the hospital?

    _____

2. What did the doctors and nurses encourage him to do?

    _____

3. What two things did the group help Andy to do?

    a. _____

    b. _____

4. What three positive things have happened to Andy?

    a. _____

    b. _____

    c. _____

5. How does Andy feel about himself?

    _____

C.   As the story of Andy D. shows, lotteries cost more than just the small change in people's pocket. Compulsive lottery gamblers will spend money, even steal money, to buy lottery tickets. This kind of addiction can lead to financial problems like bankruptcy and job loss, health problems such as depression and suicide, and social problems like divorce and jail time for people who end up in court. The social cost of compulsive lottery gamblers can only be estimated. Some think the total amount could reach into the billions of dollars in the United States. In North America, the number of lotteries is increasing. Governments use this money to pay for things like education. The question remains: Are lotteries a good way for governments to raise money?

1. What are two things that compulsive lottery gamblers will do to buy tickets?

   a. _____

   b. _____

2. What are three types of problems that compulsive lottery gamblers can have? Give one example of each.

Type	*Example*
a. _____	_____
b. _____	_____
c. _____	_____

3. What is the total cost to society of each person addicted to gambling?

   _____

4. What question are people asking about lotteries?

   _____

Compare answers with your partner. Try to agree on the same answer. Look back at the reading if you disagree.

RECAPPING THE STORY

List the facts of the story in note form.

Beating the Odds
- Andy D's life as a lottery gambler
  successful businessman and restaurant owner
  married and had two children
  problem: loved to gamble

_____

_____

_____

_____

_____

_____

_____

_____

Work with a partner who took notes about the same story. Take turns explaining several of the facts to each other. Check to make sure that you both have the same information. Add any facts you didn't note. Correct any facts you need to.

REACTING TO THE STORY

Share your ideas about these questions with a partner.

1. What caused Andy D's problems?
2. How did he solve his problems?
3. Does this story show the positive or the negative side of lotteries?

_____

After Reading

RETELLING THE STORY

Work with a partner who took notes about the other story. Use your notes to retell the information.

COMPARING THE STORIES

Answer these questions based on the information from both stories.

1. What are the similarities and differences in the problems of the people in these two stories?
2. Is winning the lottery a solution to people's financial problems?
3. Are lotteries good or bad for society?

Vocabulary Building

MATCHING MEANINGS

Match each phrase in Column A with the word or phrase that is the closest in meaning in Column B. Remember that sometimes when certain verbs and prepositions are combined they have special meanings.

Column A	Column B
_____ 1. give up	a. continue
_____ 2. win back	b. return
_____ 3. move in	c. trust
_____ 4. pay for	d. finish paying
_____ 5. give back	e. remove
_____ 6. pay off	f. stop trying
_____ 7. end up	g. regain
_____ 8. go on	h. conclude
_____ 9. take away	i. buy
_____10. believe in	j. occupy a home

Work with a partner to check your answers.

SYNONYMS

Circle the word that has the closest meaning to the word in bold.

1. **allow**   punish   put   prohibit   permit

2. **leave**   enter   exit   excite   exhibit

3. **promise**   come   command   commit   combine

4. **realize**   underestimate   undergo   understand   underdone

5. **spend**   use for   use up   use instead   use with

Work with a partner to check your answers.

Expanding Your Language

REACTION WRITING

Think about the topic of lotteries and their effect on people. Are lotteries good or bad for society? Write about your ideas and any examples that you know of. For example, you can write about the different places where there are lotteries. What success and failure stories do you know?

SPEAKING

A. Talk It Out: Work with a partner and tell each other about the ideas you wrote about. Begin by asking, "How do lotteries affect people in positive and negative ways?" Ask questions to find out more about your partner's ideas.

B. Survey: Write four or five questions to survey some of your classmates and find out what they think about the role of lotteries in society. To review how to write a survey, see the example on page 87.

CHAPTER 9

The Future of Money

Chapter Openers

DISCUSSION QUESTIONS

Think about these questions. Share your ideas with a partner or with a small group.

1. How do you like to pay for things: with cash, with a credit card, with a bank card, or by check?

2. a. What are some purchases you can't use a credit card or a bank card to make?

   b. What are some purchases you need a credit card or a bank card to make?

3. What are the benefits and dangers of using a bank card or a credit card to buy things?

4. Do you think that in the future you will use cash as much as or less than you do now?

Exploring and Understanding Reading

PREDICTING

Circle T for true and F for false. Guess the answers to questions you are not sure of.

1. T F   Bank cards, or debit cards, can be used to buy items like gas, movie tickets, and groceries.

2. T F   Most workers receive their paychecks at work.

3. T F   The government spends money every year to replace worn-out or damaged bills.

4. T F   When people use bank cards to buy things, they spend more than if they paid in cash.

5. T F   If your bank card is stolen, thieves can use it to take money from your bank account.

Work with a partner. Compare your answers. You don't have to agree, but explain your reasons as completely as possible. After you finish reading, return to these questions and answer them based on the information you read.

SKIMMING

Read the selection quickly and choose the statement that best expresses the general idea of the reading.

a. People use bank cards to purchase more of the things they need.

b. There are advantages and disadvantages in using bank cards instead of cash.

c. People who use bank cards instead of money get into debt more easily.

How Will You Be Paying?

A. In North America, it seems that we need money less and less these days. The amount of money, or currency as it is called, in circulation in the United States today is about $400 billion. But, since total yearly money exchanges amount to more than $4 trillion dollars, we have to wonder why there is so little money in circulation. It turns out that one of the main reasons there is so little cash today is that Americans are making more and more business and banking transactions electronically. Today money is just information that is moved around by the computers that we depend on for so much in our society.

B. We're paying for more and more things electronically. Bank cards can be used to pay for our gas, buy our movie tickets, and even purchase our groceries. In some places you can even use a card to pay for a taxi. You need a credit card to reserve a hotel room or rent a car. You can pay your bills from your home computer or at your banking machine (ATM) without ever using cash or writing a check. Since 1986, the number of electronic transfers from bank accounts has risen almost 200 percent. During this time, the number of check and cash transactions rose only 17 percent. In the past most workers received their paychecks at work. Now more than a third of all U.S. workers have their paychecks deposited directly into their accounts.

C. There are many advantages to using cards instead of money. You can buy things without having to bother to go to the bank first. But large institutions like the banks, governments, and businesses benefit the most from electronic banking. As of 1993, there were about 12 billion pieces of U.S. paper money in circulation. Paper money wears out or is damaged over time, so the U.S. government has to spend about $200 million a year to replace it. Businesses have to spend time to count, store, and protect the money that is brought in. It costs a bank more money in time and administration to process checks than to carry out electronic transactions. In 1993 the U.S. government saved $133 million by paying 47 percent of its bills by computer. All of these savings in time and dollars add up.

D. Of course, using cards instead of cash is not worry free. You sometimes have to pay a small service charge when you buy something with your card. And cards are easy to lose. There are a lot of cards left at the supermarket checkout counter. Some banks issue a card that doesn't need a PIN, or personal identification number, to make purchases. If such a card is stolen, thieves can quickly make charges on your account before you realize the card is gone. But, beyond safety, money management experts are worried about the effect of cards on people's attitudes toward money. It is easier to give in to the impulse to buy when you can just pull out your card to make a purchase. It is easier to lose track of the amount of money and overspend when you use a bank card. If you're a spender by nature, you could get into debt more easily. Clearly, there is a lot to be careful about when it comes to using cards instead of money.

E. Will we give up money for good and use "smart cards" in the future? The time when we won't need to carry money at all may be coming sooner than we think. But will this make our financial lives easier or not?

RECOGNIZING SUB-POINTS

Circle S if the statement is a sub-point or D if the statement is a detail.

■ *READING TIP:*
Noticing that some information is more general (sub-points of the main idea) than other information (the details), is an important critical reading skill.

1. S   D   Since 1986, the number of electronic transfers from bank accounts has risen almost 200 percent.

2. S   D   We're paying for more and more things electronically.

3. S   D   But the real benefits of electronic transactions are the savings to large institutions like banks, governments, and businesses.

4. S   D   As of 1993, there were about 12 billion pieces of U.S. paper money in circulation.

5. S   D   Another worry is losing your card.

6. S   D   It is easier to lose track of the amount of money you have when you use a bank card.

After Reading

REACTING TO THE STORY

Decide your opinion about the following statement:

Do electronic money transactions make us more or less independent:
a. on a personal level?
b. on a social level?

Give as many reasons and examples for your opinion as you can. Discuss your ideas with others in a small group. Share your ideas with your classmates.

APPLYING THE INFORMATION: CONTRASTING IDEAS

In Chapter 8, in the Reading "Beating the Odds" the writer uses the expression "spare change." Spare change is the money we carry in our wallet or leave on our desk. Find out how one person in the United States is making use of the money we sometimes overlook.

Pennies from Heaven

Those pennies on top of your dresser may be worth more than you think.

A Chicago nun who asked folks to send in their pennies has racked up a whopping $37,000—and the penny pot is still growing.

Sister Eileen says she began by asking friends, family, and former students for their unwanted pennies in order to reach her original goal of raising $20,000—or 2 million pennies.

But now Sister Eileen says she's shooting for enough pennies to pay for a new pickup truck, which the parish can use to retrieve bulkier donated items.

She says there are so many worthy causes out there that people have trouble deciding who to give their dollars to.

But, when it comes to pennies, Sister Eileen says most folks consider them a nuisance and just want to get rid of them.

DISCUSSION QUESTIONS

Discuss the following questions with a partner or with a small group.

1. Why is Sister Eileen asking people to send her their pennies?
2. Has her project been successful?
3. What does Sister Eileen say about people's attitude toward pennies?
4. What would happen to this kind of project in the age of electronic money?

Vocabulary Building

EXPRESSIONS

A. Match each expression in Column A with its meaning in Column B.

Column A	Column B
_____ 1. rack up	a. throw away
_____ 2. get rid of	b. overuse
_____ 3. shoot for	c. forget
_____ 4. wear out	d. accumulate
_____ 5. lose track of	e. try to get

B. Use each expression in a sentence of your own. Write your sentences on a separate paper. Work with a partner and take turns reading your sentences.

VOCABULARY IN CONTEXT

Complete each sentence with one of the words in the list. Use your understanding of one part of the sentence to help you guess the word that is missing. Circle the words that helped you decide your answer.

a. cost   e. process   h. rent

b. count   f. received   i. risen

c. deposit   g. reduce   j. stolen

d. give

1. You should call the bank if your card is lost or

   _____ and cancel the card immediately.

2. The employees had the company _____ their pay checks directly into their accounts.

3. After three weeks she finally _____ the money that they owed her.

4. The bank told her that it would take several days to

   _____ the checks and put the money into her account.

5. The auto rental company said she needed a credit card to

   _____ a car for the weekend.

6. It is a good idea to _____ the amount of money you owe on your credit card.

7. If you _____ all the money on my dresser, I have about fifteen dollars to spend.

8. Is it too late to _____ you the money to buy a ticket for tonight's concert?

9. The restaurant looked expensive, but she told me the meal

   wouldn't _____ a lot of money.

10. She said the price had _____ from $50 to $100 in just three years.

Work with a partner and take turns reading your completed sentences.

Expanding Your Language

SPEAKING

A. Talk It Out: Work with a partner or with a small group of people from different countries. Find out how people do banking, make purchases, and pay bills in other places. Find out about people's attitudes toward money. Is it common for people to carry cash with them or to use credit cards? Do people think it's important to keep money in the bank? Ask questions to find out more about your partner's ideas.

B. Debate: In the future we won't need to use cash; money will be a thing of the past. Do you agree or disagree with this statement? Work with a partner to think of and present reasons in favor of or against this statement. Prepare to talk for one to two minutes about your ideas. Practice explaining your point of view with your partner. When you are ready, present your point of view to someone who has a different argument. Listen carefully and ask your partner who has an opposing view questions about the information. Share your ideas with your classmates.

WRITING

A. Topic Writing: Using the information in this chapter reading, write about the advantages and disadvantages of using cards instead of cash. Use examples of your own to help you explain your ideas.

B. Reaction Writing: What does the story about Sister Eileen show you about attitudes toward money? Write about the different attitudes toward money that people have. Give as many details as possible.

Read On: Taking It Further

NEWSPAPER ARTICLES

▪ READING TIP:
Don't forget to write your reading journal and add vocabulary log entries to your notebook.

Check the newspaper over a few days and find an interesting article about lotteries or other money-related topics. Take notes as you did for the reading in Chapter 8, pages 92 or 97. Prepare to present the information to a partner or a small group.

WORD PLAY

A Spelling Game. You can use vocabulary from the chapter readings to play this game. Think of a pair of words, like *loan* and *number*. The last letter of *loan* is the first letter of *number*. Select a partner and follow these rules to play the game.

1. Make your list of seven to ten words from the readings that can be paired with another word.
2. Give your partner the first word to spell.
3. Your partner spells the word and must select a new word that begins with the last letter of the word spelled (one-minute time limit). If your partner can't find a word, you supply the answer.
4. Continue to take turns until time is called by the teacher (after approximately 10–15 minutes).
5. The person who correctly chooses and spells the most words wins.

UNIT 4

Protecting Nature

One Generation Goes, Another Generation Comes,
But the Earth Remains Forever.

—ECCLESIASTES 1.4

Introducing the Topics

People have had an enormous effect on the natural world. Today, we know that we have to protect the natural world. This unit is about the ways we are making a difference in the struggle to protect nature. In Chapter 10 you will find out what modern-day zoos are doing to save animals. Chapter 11 introduces you to the controversy about bringing wolves back to Yellowstone National Park. Chapter 12 examines ways to protect our future supplies of fresh water.

Points of Interest

DESCRIPTIONS

Think about these statements. Share your ideas with a partner or in a small group.

1. What are some natural areas outdoors that you like, for example, beaches, forests, lakes, mountains, deserts, or rivers? Describe what is special about these wilderness areas. What do you like to do in these places?

2. Describe wild animals that you find interesting. Describe the places you would see these animals.

3. Describe what your feelings are about being outdoors.

QUESTIONNAIRE

Do you think we need to protect the natural world more today than in the past? Read the following list of important reasons to protect nature. Check those that are important to you. Mark their order of importance from 1 (very important) to 5 (least important). Add any ideas of your own.

Reasons to Protect Nature   *Importance*

_____ Because we can relax when we're outdoors   _____

_____ Because it's important to future generations   _____

_____ Because we want to preserve the beauty of nature   _____

_____ Because it's good for the economy   _____

_____ Because it's important for science understanding   _____

_____ Because it could be dangerous if we don't protect it _____

Other: _____   _____

Share your ideas with a partner or with a small group.

CHAPTER 10

Something's Happening at the Zoos

Chapter Openers

DISCUSSION QUESTIONS

Think about these questions. Share your ideas with a partner or with a small group.

1. What kind of animals are in the zoo?
2. What kind of jobs do people do at the zoo?
3. Are zoos good places for animals? Should animals be kept there?
4. Should wild animals be caught and brought to a zoo?

Exploring and Understanding Reading

In the interview you will get a picture of the kind of work zoos do.

PERSONALIZING

Imagine that you were going to interview the director of a zoo in a large city. Write four questions that you might ask.

1. _____

2. _____

3. _____

4. _____

Interview with a Zoo Director

SKIMMING

Quickly read the interview and circle the correct answer.

The zoo director
a. favors the work done in modern zoos.
b. opposes the work done in modern zoos.
c. wants to change the work done in modern zoos.

Andrew McTagger is the director of a zoo located in a large North American city. In this interview he explains the type of work that is done in today's modern zoos.

Q: What was the purpose of the first modern zoos?

A: Well, the first zoos were the only places where most people could really see wild animals.

Q: And today that's changed, right?

A: Well, on the one hand, zoos are still the only places where most people can see these animals live and up close. Seeing an animal, even in the zoo, touches people, especially young people. Most zoos today have great educational exhibits. On the other hand, now we can watch TV programs that show how animals live in the wild.

Q: Do you think that zoos are good places for wild animals to live?

A: Well, in some ways, yes. First of all, we can build better cages for the animals. Today cages are called enclosures. In the bear's enclosure, for example, we re-create the forest with different kinds of plants, and tree trunks, rocks, and waterfalls.

Q: Do you think the animal feels as if it were right at home?

A: No, probably not. But we try to do as much as we can. What's really different is that today we look after the animal's psychological and physical needs. For example, we create places where they can be private and hide away from people. We put in big rocks with spaces to crawl into, or trees to go behind.

Q: What are some other ways that you try to look after the animals' psychological health?

A: We try to give them work to do.

Q: What do you mean by work?

A: In the wild, animals spend most all of their time—95 percent of it—looking for food. So we try to find ways to make the animals work for their food. We put seeds and other food pieces in different parts of their enclosure so that they have to look for the food. Take the polar bears, for example. We freeze the fish pieces in ice cubes so the animals have to break the ice to get the food. We don't want their feeding schedule to be boring so we bring the food at different times of the day.

Q: Does this make a difference?

A: Yes, the animals spend much more time walking around, looking for pieces of food and exploring their enclosure. I'll tell you the story of what happened at one zoo. This zoo had a wild Asian cat that spent all its time sleeping, so they decided to give the animal a challenge. They put its food high up in the cage. Today, that cat is awake and jumping to get the food. It will even jump 15 feet to bring down its dinner.

Q: What are the health problems of keeping wild animals in zoos?

A: Well, there are many problems. First of all, people still try to give food to the animals or throw things into the animals' cages that can harm them, like plastic wrappers or candy. The animals can choke on some of these things. A second problem is that animals can get sick easily from being in contact with people. A human cold virus can be very dangerous and if the animal doesn't have any immunity to that virus, it will get very sick!

Q: What do you think is the most important job that zoos have to do today?

A: Conservation work.

Q: What do you mean by that, saving animals?

A: Exactly. We can help animals that are endangered in the wild to reproduce in the safety of zoos. And then the zoos can return these animals to the wild.

Q: Is it important for zoos to do this work?

A: It's very important. Don't forget it's estimated that about 200 to 300 animals in the wild become extinct every year; and that number is increasing in rate. I think that zoos have an important part to play in saving animals from extinction. This is the future role of zoos in North America.

Q: Are there any difficulties doing this work?

A: The zoo has to see that the animal can survive before it is returned to its natural habitat. For example, they have to decide if the animal can hunt for its own food in the wild. And it's very expensive work so only a very few zoos can pay for these repopulation programs.

UNDERSTANDING EXPLANATIONS

Look for the information to answer these questions. Give examples to explain the answer.

■ *READING TIP:*
In English a common way to explain what you mean is to give an example. Special words, including for example, for instance, like, or such as, are used to introduce examples. The information in examples can help you to understand the general idea.

1. How do zoos build better cages or enclosures for the animals?

_____

2. What are two special ways the zoos can make it interesting for the animals to find food?

    a. _____

    b. _____

3. What kind of health problems can be caused by people?

    a. _____

    b. _____

4. What is one example of the work a zoo is doing to save wild animals?

    _____

5. What does a zoo have to know before returning an animal to the wild?

    _____

Compare answers with your partner. Try to agree on the same answer. Check the reading to confirm your answers.

NOTE-TAKING: LISTING ADVANTAGES

List four facts that are positive points about zoos.

1. _____

    _____

2. _____

    _____

3. _____

    _____

4. _____

    _____

Work with a partner and take turns comparing the facts you chose. Work with your partner to add as many facts as possible to your list. Check your facts with your classmates.

After Reading

APPLYING THE INFORMATION: MAKING A DECISION

Read this story about Keiko, the captured killer whale, and use what you know about zoo animals to help you make a decision in this case.

Should Keiko the Whale Be Set Free?

Keiko is an orca, or killer whale, who was captured in the North Atlantic Ocean in 1979 at the age of one or two. This killer whale became famous as the star of the 1993 movie *Free Willy*. After the movie, Keiko was moved to a small tank in an amusement park in Mexico City. Here in the warm-water climate and without enough room to move, Keiko became sick. His skin was covered with sores, and he was not gaining enough weight. When people learned what had happened to Keiko, they formed a foundation, the Free Willy Keiko Foundation, that raised money to bring the whale to the cold-water climate of Oregon on the West Coast of the United States.

In 1995 Keiko arrived at the Oregon Coast Aquarium. Keiko's skin healed and he gained almost 2,000 pounds. Keiko was the "star" of the aquarium. After Keiko arrived, the attendance at the aquarium has doubled to 1.3 million. Two years after his arrival, the Foundation announced that it thought Keiko was healthy enough to be released back into the wild. But the aquarium directors disagreed. They said that Keiko was not well enough to be released and, more important, that they didn't think Keiko could ever survive in the wild. According to the aquarium directors, Keiko is so used to people that he does not hunt for food on his own. The Foundation argued that Keiko should be brought to a seawater enclosure on the North Atlantic coast. In August 1998, Keiko was moved to an enclosure in the waters off Iceland. The plan is to release Keiko back into the wild. Many people are worried about this decision.

Do you think that Keiko can survive in the wild? What do you think the arguments are for releasing Keiko? What are the arguments against releasing Keiko? What should be done in cases like this?

To answer these questions, follow these steps:

1. Make a list of the reasons for and against releasing Keiko into the wild.
2. Get together with a small group of people who share your opinion and complete your list of reasons.
3. Check your list with your teacher and then present your ideas to some classmates who prepared the opposing argument.
4. In your group, try to reach agreement about the decision that should be made.
5. Report your decision to the class. Explain the reasons for the decision.

Vocabulary Building

VOCABULARY IN CONTEXT: JIGSAW SENTENCES

Match the beginning of the sentence in Column A with the best completion of the sentence in Column B.

Column A

_____ 1. It's estimated that

_____ 2. The enclosures are

_____ 3. They tried to hide the food

Column B

a. in ice cubes or in holes in trees.

b. 200–300 animals become extinct annually.

c. larger and more natural than in the past.

ADJECTIVES

Complete each sentence with one of the words in the list. Use your understanding of one part of the sentence to help you guess the missing word. Circle the words that helped you decide your answer.

a. dangerous   c. expensive   e. wild
b. educational   d. psychological

1. At the zoo, people can see _____ animals that they wouldn't see every day.

2. Zoos are interested in the animal's physical and

 _____ health.

3. It is difficult to pay for conservation work because it is so

 _____ .

4. A human cold virus is _____ because it can make an animal very sick.

5. Zoos have many _____ exhibits so people can learn more about the animals.

Check your answers. Work with a partner and take turns reading the completed sentences.

Expanding Your Language

WRITING

A. Explaining Advantages: Use the information from your list of facts to write about the advantages of today's zoos. Give examples to explain your ideas.

B. Point of View: Write about the case of Keiko, the captive killer whale. Explain what you know about the case and give your opinion about what you think is best for Keiko.

SPEAKING: ROLE-PLAY

Work with a partner. Take the roles of the aquarium director and a newspaper reporter. Write out an interview about the fate of Keiko, the captive killer whale or about a similar case. Using the interview with the zoo director as an example, prepare questions and answers. Use your lines to act out the role, but do not try to memorize what you have written. Be creative.

CHAPTER 11

The Return of the Wolves

Chapter Openers

DISCUSSION QUESTIONS

Think about the following questions. Share your ideas with a partner or with a small group.

1. What do you know or think about wolves?
    a. What do wolves look and act like?
    b. Where do wolves live?
    c. What do wolves like to eat?
    d. What stories do people tell about wolves?
2. What positive or negative feelings do you have about wolves?

PAIRED READINGS

Choose one of the readings. Work with a partner who is reading the same story.

■ ■
_____

Reading 1:
Wolves in Yellowstone National Park

SKIMMING

Read the selection and circle the answer to the following question:

Is everyone in favor of returning wolves to Yellowstone National Park?

Yes   No

Work with a partner. Explain the reasons for your answer. Answer the questions after each paragraph. Underline the words in the reading that support the answer.

A. Yellowstone National Park is a wilderness area located in the west of the United States. The Rocky Mountains run through the park. The park has 2.3 million acres of mountains, river valleys, and forests. Every year visitors come here to see one of the last completely wild places in the United States. The park today is home to many wild animals, such as elk, buffalo, and bear. In the past it was also home to another wild animal—the gray wolf. There used to be many wolves in the United States. In fact, it is estimated that in the 1600s gray wolf populations could be found in areas from northern Mexico to Greenland. But wolves were killed when people moved in and settled the United States, so that by 1870 the gray wolf population was falling rapidly. In the 1920s the last gray wolves were hunted down and completely eliminated from Yellowstone National Park. Since that time, environmentalists have worked to see the return of wolves to Yellowstone National Park. In 1973, the U.S. government passed a law that made it possible to return wolves to Yellowstone. In 1982 the U.S. Fish and Wildlife Service first suggested a plan to move ten breeding pairs of wolves to the park. Years of consultation and discussion followed the introduction of this controversial plan. Some people argued in favor and some against the return of the wolves.

1. Where is Yellowstone National Park located? How large is it?

   _____

   _____

2. What kind of animals can you find in the park? What can't you find there?

   _____

   _____

3. What area did gray wolves inhabit in the 1600s?

   _____

   _____

4. What happened to gray wolves in the United States and in Yellowstone National Park by 1920?

   _____

   _____

5. What happened in the 1970s to make it possible to return wolves to Yellowstone? What happened in the 1980s?

   a. 1970s _____

   b. 1980s _____

B.   In 1995, seventeen wolves captured in Canada were released into Yellowstone Park. Some Canadians were unhappy about the removal of these animals from their natural habitat. They were worried that the animals might die as a result of the move. They were also worried that the wolves would be killed by hunters or ranchers in the United States. On the other hand, the hunters are concerned that wolves will prey on the elk and kill so many that there won't be enough left for them to hunt. Ranchers and farmers who live in the area near Yellowstone argue against returning wolves to the area. From their point of view, these wolves are dangerous because they will hunt their livestock, the cattle and sheep that feed in pastures next to the park. Some ranchers and farmers say that wolves could attack small children and domestic animals such as dogs who live near the park. Many people simply feel that the federal government should not be spending the taxpayers' dollars to return the gray wolves to Yellowstone.

1. What happened in 1996?

   _____

   _____

2. Why were some Canadians unhappy about the removal of the wolves?

   a. _____

   b. _____

3. What are three reasons that hunters, ranchers, and farmers don't want wolves returned to Yellowstone National Park?

   a. _____

   b. _____

   c. _____

C.   Those who are in favor of bringing the wolves back to Yellowstone have their arguments. Biologists say that wolves play an important part in the ecosystem of this wilderness area. Through their hunting they remove the weak and diseased members of the elk and deer populations. They keep the populations from growing too large. Naturalists believe the wolves are an essential part of the wilderness. And they are the only part of the ecosystem that is missing from the Yellowstone area. Naturalists want to restore Yellowstone to the way it was before Columbus set foot in America in 1492. They want visitors to the park to have the experience of hearing wolves howl at night—an experience many describe as the best the wilderness has to offer.

1. What are three reasons that people want wolves returned to Yellowstone National Park?

    a. _____

    b. _____

    c. _____

2. What experience do naturalists want park visitors to have?

    _____

    _____

Compare answers with your partner. Try to agree on the same answer. Look back at the reading if you disagree.

RECAPPING THE INFORMATION: HIGHLIGHTING

■ *READING TIP:*
Highlighting is a useful strategy for finding and remembering facts and important ideas you read. To highlight, use a colored highlighting pen to mark information. Be careful to mark only the words and phrases that you want to stand out—not the whole sentence. Use the underlining you did to answer the scanning questions to help you locate the correct information to highlight.

A. Highlight the facts you read about wolves relating to these ideas:

1. History of Wolves in Yellowstone
2. The Wolves in Yellowstone Today

B. Pair Work: Compare your highlighting with your partner's. Add any highlighting you need to. Using the highlighting, tell the important facts of the story.

REACTING TO THE INFORMATION

Discuss these questions with a partner.

1. What facts do you think would convince the people who oppose the return of wolves to Yellowstone National Park to change their minds?

2. Do you think the advantages of reintroducing wolves to Yellowstone are greater than the disadvantages?

■ ■

Reading 2: The Unknown Lives of Wolves

SKIMMING

Read the selection and circle the answer to the following question:

Do people have the same attitude toward wolves?

Yes   No

Work with a partner. Explain the reasons for your answer.

Answer the questions after each paragraph. Underline the words in the reading that support the answer.

A.   Wolves are among the most mysterious of wild animals that live in North America. They are strong animals with powerful jaws. They've been known to track, or follow, animals for many miles. But, despite the popular image, wolves do not needlessly attack and kill other animals. In one study of wolf behavior, scientists recorded wolves following moose 131 times. In these hunts, wolves attacked only 7 times and killed only 6 times. Animals can and do defend themselves against wolves. Wolves travel in small groups called "packs." On average, a pack is made up of a dominant female and a dominant male, several males and females, and pups (wolf babies) that are raised by all the adults. Again, contrary to popular belief, the pack is led not by the dominant male but by the dominant female. The females mark the pack's territory. Often the females break the snow and lead the pack on the hunt.

1. What two features show the strength of wolves?

   a. _____

   b. _____

2. What facts show that wolves do not needlessly attack and kill other animals?

   a. _____

   b. _____

   c. _____

3. What animals make up a wolf pack? Who is the leader of the pack?

   _____

   _____

B.   Some think of wolves as dangerous killers. But, while other wild animals like bears and mountain lions have attacked and killed people, there are no records of any healthy wolves attacking people in North America. There are a few reports of wolves scratching or biting people, but no reports of serious injuries. However, wolves will attack dogs and other domestic pets. They will also attack livestock such as cattle or sheep. On average, wolves kill as many as three cattle per thousand each year. When wolves regularly attack livestock, rangers capture and remove them. If the wolves return, they are removed and killed. In Minnesota, 1,200 wolves live in an area where there is ranching. The government pays ranchers if any of their cows or sheep are killed by wolves. The highest amount paid in any one year to ranchers for animals killed by wolves was $21,000. As part of the plan for the reintroduction of wolves to Yellowstone National Park in Montana, ranchers could shoot wolves that kill or wound their livestock as long as they report the shooting within twenty-four hours and can provide physical evidence that an attack took place.

1. What facts do we know about wolf attacks on people?

   a. _____

   b. _____

2. What facts do we know about wolf attacks on animals?

   a. _____

   b. _____

3. What will rangers do when wolves attack livestock?

   _____

4. What happens to wolves that return to attack livestock?

   _____

5. What facts show that ranchers can be protected against losses caused by wolves?

   _____

   _____

C.   The wolves that have recently been reintroduced to Yellowstone National Park are part of an experiment. Researchers want to study the effect of returning wolves on the ecology of Yellowstone to see if the area would benefit from the reintroduction or if it would damage the balance of nature. Ranchers, farmers, and hunters object to the reintroduction of wolves from Canada to the United States. In November 1997 a U.S. federal judge ordered the Canadian wolves to be removed from Yellowstone. That order has not been carried out. Researchers say that, so far, studies show that the return of the wolves has benefited the environment of the park. The number of wolves has increased to 97 from the 33 that were introduced in 1995 and 1996. The wolves have killed coyotes and elk and, as a result, a greater variety of other animals, like bears, rodents, hawks, and bald eagles that live off dead meat, have survived in the park. But, more time is needed to see if there are proven benefits and if the wolves will be allowed to stay.

1. What do researchers want to study?

_____

_____

2. Who objects to the reintroduction of wolves?

_____

_____

3. What order did a federal judge give?

_____

_____

4. By how much has the population of wolves increased?

_____

_____

5. What effect has the wolf population had on the wildlife in the park?

_____

_____

6. What will happen next?

_____

_____

Compare answers with your partner. Try to agree on the same answer. Look back at the reading if you disagree.

RECAPPING THE INFORMATION: HIGHLIGHTING

A. Highlight the facts of these ideas about wolves:

■ *READING TIP:*
See page 125 for tips
on highlighting.

1. Characteristics of Wolves
2. Wolves in Yellowstone Today

B. Pair Work: Compare your highlighting with your partner's. Highlight any important facts you didn't include. Using the highlighting, tell the important facts of the story.

REACTING TO THE INFORMATION

Discuss these questions with a partner.

1. Do the facts show that wolves are dangerous to other animals and humans?
2. Can wolves be good for the environment of Yellowstone National Park?
3. Do you think Canadian wolves should be allowed to stay in Yellowstone National Park? Why or why not?

After Reading

RETELLING THE INFORMATION

Work with a partner who took notes about the other story. Use your notes to retell the information.

Quickly tell your partner about the important facts you highlighted. Explain the ideas clearly in your own words. Encourage your partner to ask questions about the information or note some of the important facts you explain. Together discuss the questions in "Reacting to the Information."

APPLYING THE INFORMATION: USING FACTS TO MAKE AN ARGUMENT

A court order was issued in December 1997 to remove the Canadian wolves from Yellowstone National Park and return them to Canada. There were objections to this decision. Another, higher court, overturned the first decision. Now people are waiting to see what the final decision on keeping the wolves in Yellowstone will be.

What decision would you want the court to make? What facts can you use to support your opinion?

To prepare and present your argument, complete the following steps:

1. Choose an argument either for or against allowing Canadian wolves to remain in Yellowstone National Park.
2. Work together in a small group of people who share your opinion. Include people who prepared both readings in the group. Use the facts from both readings to find support for your argument. Add facts of your own to make your arguments stronger.
3. Make a final list of all the facts you can use. When you have completed your list, practice presenting your arguments with a partner.
4. Work with a partner who prepared the opposite argument. Take two minutes each to present your case. Listen to your partner's argument. Write the facts of your partner's argument in note form.
5. With your classmates, make a list of all the arguments for and against keeping the wolves in Yellowstone. Ask and answer any questions about the facts of the case. As a class, try to agree on what you think the court decision should be.

Vocabulary Building

WORD FORMS

In English, the form of a word can be changed. One of the ways is to add a special suffix, or word ending. The suffix *-tion, -ion,* or *-sion* can be added to certain verbs to form nouns.

Choose the correct word to complete the sentences. Use your knowledge of grammar rules to help you make the right choice.

1. consult / consultation

    a. The ranchers wanted to know if the government would

       _____ with them.

    b. They made a plan to meet ranchers and be available for

       _____ with them.

2. discuss / discussion

    a. They decided that a lot of _____ was needed to find out people's opinions.

    b. They decided that they would _____ their difference of opinion.

3. eliminate / elimination

    a. The original settlers wanted to see the total

       _____ of the wolf population.

    b. The original settlers wanted to _____ wolves because they thought they were dangerous.

4. oppose / opposition

    a. They told the government they would _____ this plan.

    b. They told the government there was a lot of

       _____ to this plan.

5. introduce / introduction

    a. They planned for the _____ of six pairs of animals into the park.

    b. They planned to _____ six pairs of animals into the park.

Work with a partner and take turns reading your sentences.

Expanding Your Language

WRITING

A. Reporting. Use the information from your reading, discussions, and the argument presentation to write about the wolves in Yellowstone Park. Write as much as you can on the topic. Follow the steps for outlining in the activity on page 12.

B. Reacting. Give your opinion about what the courts should decide about returning the wolves to Canada. Give as many reasons as possible to support your opinion.

SPEAKING

A. Two-Minute Taped Talk. Using your own ideas and the information in this chapter, choose a topic to present on the wolves of Yellowstone Park. Plan to speak for two to three minutes on the topic. Make a short outline of your ideas in note form. Practice your talk a few times before you record. Record your talk on tape and give it to your teacher for feedback.

B. Role-play: Interviewing. Role-play a radio interview with a partner. One person takes the role of the expert; the other takes the role of the reporter. Look back at the interview of a zoo director on pages 114–115. Work with a partner to prepare five to seven questions and answers about the wolves in Yellowstone National Park. Together write out what you will say in the interview. Do not try to memorize your answers. Speak as naturally and completely as possible. Present your interview to another pair in your class or tape it for your teacher.

Protecting Water Resources

Chapter Openers

SURVEYS: LISTING IDEAS

A. Work with a partner or with a small group. Make a list of the top ten reasons why people need to have supplies of fresh water.

WATER NEEDS SURVEY

Example: 1. Water to drink   6. _____

             2. _____   7. _____

             3. _____   8. _____

             4. _____   9. _____

             5. _____   10. _____

B. Decide the five most important reasons and their order of importance. Discuss your ideas about these questions with a partner or with a small group.

1. Where does your water supply come from?
2. Have you ever had to reduce the amount of water you use? When?
3. Do you think we will need to ration (use only a specific amount of) water in the future?
4. Are there places where water has disappeared or been polluted?
5. What can be done to keep water clean?
6. How would your life change if there wasn't enough water?

OPINIONS: THINKING ABOUT PROBLEMS AND SOLUTIONS

Where in the world is water supply a problem?

How could water be supplied to these areas?

Give your opinion whether each of the following methods is possible or not. Circle P (possible) or I (impossible). Be prepared to talk about the details of these proposed methods: where, how, when, who, and what.

P   I   Desalination (taking salt out of ocean water or seawater)

P   I   Pumping water out of aquifers (lakes under the ground)

P   I   Importing water from places that have enough of a supply

P   I   Transporting icebergs from the polar caps

P   I   Requiring people who use too much water to pay or share with people who have too little of their own

P   I   Recycling wastewater for needs like watering the garden.

Exploring and Understanding Reading

PREVIEWING GRAPHIC INFORMATION

This reading is about possible problems with the world's water supply. There are some charts and diagrams that present information related to the topic in the reading. Their purpose is to help the reader to get information visually. Before you begin to read, preview the article by looking at this graphic information. Read the text titles and subtitles and answer the following questions:

1. What kind of information will I get out of this reading?
   a. Factual information
   b. Personal opinion
   c. Stories about people

2. What is the overall topic of this reading?
   a. Possible ways to solve the problem of water shortages in the world
   b. Ways to use water for farming
   c. Why it's not a good idea to use too much groundwater

Global Water Shortages

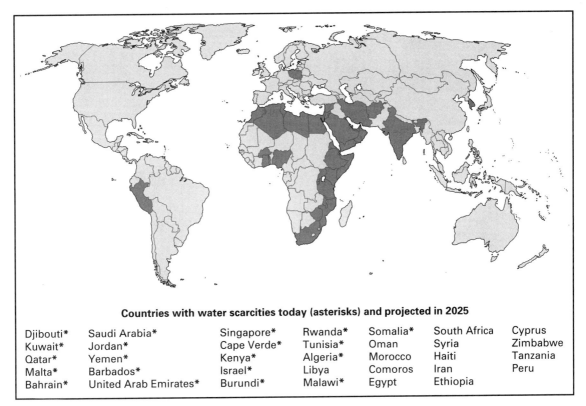

Countries with water scarcities today (asterisks) and projected in 2025

Djibouti*	Saudi Arabia*	Singapore*	Rwanda*	Somalia*	South Africa	Cyprus
Kuwait*	Jordan*	Cape Verde*	Tunisia*	Oman	Syria	Zimbabwe
Qatar*	Yemen*	Kenya*	Algeria*	Morocco	Haiti	Tanzania
Malta*	Barbados*	Israel*	Libya	Comoros	Iran	Peru
Bahrain*	United Arab Emirates*	Burundi*	Malawi*	Egypt	Ethiopia	

Global Water Shortages According to the World Bank, some twenty countries don't have enough renewable water today. By 2025, the situation in these countries will be worse and 14 other countries will have water supply problems.

Note: Countries that have less than 1,000 cubic meters of water per capita per year fall into the category "water scarce." Water that comes from rain or rivers is called renewable water.

Will the Earth run out of fresh water?

A. There are 335 million cubic miles of water on the Earth, enough to cover the United States to a depth of 93 miles. The problem is that almost 98 percent of it is salt water—unfit to drink or to use for most other human needs, such as agriculture and industry. Only about 2.5 percent of Earth's water is fresh and almost 99 percent of that small amount is locked up in the form of glaciers and permanent snow cover in the polar regions, or largely unrenewable underground aquifers.

B. Some groundwater sources can be tapped, but most of the water they contain is non-renewable, a finite resource just like oil. Once it's pumped out of the ground, it's gone forever.

C. In the final analysis, less than 1 percent of the Earth's fresh water is renewable. This is the water found in freshwater lakes and rivers. They are replenished by rainfall, river flow, and springs.

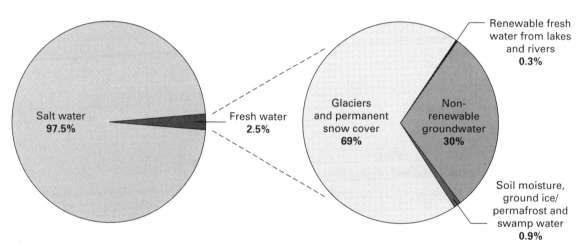

*How much water can we use? ... **Not that much!*** 75 percent of the earth is water; but we can only use about 2.5 percent. This small amount is fresh water. But 1.5 percent of the earth's fresh water is frozen in glaciers or snow, or in non-renewable lakes underground. Only 1 percent of the earth's water is renewable.

Can technology provide the solution to water shortages?

D. Given the globe's limitless quantity of salt water, desalination would seem to offer the greatest technological solution to water scarcity. But removing the salt from sea and ocean water has several drawbacks. To begin with, not all water-scarce countries have access to seawater. More important, the high cost of desalination makes it unfeasible for many developing countries, which are the most seriously affected by water shortages.

E. Most of the world's 7,500 desalination plants are in the Persian Gulf countries with access to the cheap oil supplies required to run them.

F. Some scientists see solar energy as an alternative to fossil fuels. A solar-powered desalination plant near the Red Sea port of Massawa, Ethiopia, provides enough fresh water for 500 people. But solar power is not feasible in many water-scarce countries.

G. Many proposals focus on transporting water. Some needy regions already rely heavily on water imports. The Balearic Islands of Spain, for example, receive fresh water shipped in from Scotland, while Malta is almost entirely dependent upon imported water. But shipping water is only feasible in countries with relatively strong economies. Malta's highly developed tourist trade, for example, generates enough revenue to pay for the water and food it must import.

H. More-inventive proposals to transport water on a larger scale include hauling it in huge plastic bags or towing mammoth chunks of icebergs from polar regions to the Middle East and other needy areas. "The problem is, a lot would disappear on the way through warmer waters," say the World Bank's Le Moigne. "Also, you would have to be able to stock the transported water somewhere. So there are ideas galore, but so far we do not have one that is sufficiently affordable."

As populations increase, what will countries that get their water from sources outside their borders do? Here are six countries that get more than 50 percent of their renewable water from rivers that are in other countries.

Country	Percentage of renewable water supplies originating outside borders	Years required for population to double*
Egypt	97	30.1
Netherlands	89	138.6
Cambodia	82	27.7
Syria	79	18.2
Sudan	77	22.4
Iraq	66	18.7

*Excludes migration

Source: Data from "Sustaining Water: Population and the Future of Renewable Water Supplies," Population Action International, 1993; Peter H. Gleick, ed., Water in Crisis: A Guide to the World's Fresh Water Resources, 1993.

Should water be treated as a marketable commodity?

I. Water historically has been treated as a free resource, almost like the air we breathe. But as growing consumption depletes renewable supplies in many parts of the world, water is assuming greater economic value.

J. Water resource managers point repeatedly at California's recent success in promoting conservation by all water consumers and encouraging farmers to sell their surplus water rights to cities.

K. California's Central Basin district, for example, uses wastewater that has gone through three treatment cycles for a number of non-drinking water uses, including irrigation of parks, golf courses, and freeway landscaping. The district also distributes recycled water for use in cooling towers and boilers and certain water-intensive industries such as manufacturing carpets and concrete. According to district general manager Atwater, it is the largest water-recycling project in the United States and a model for new recycling efforts in the United States and Australia.

L. "Because of the cost of water and our past droughts, industry and other large customers have tried to become much more efficient in using water and recycling waste streams," he says. "We recycle about 100 million gallons a day. It's like freeing up drinking water for a million people, so we're saving a lot of water."

SKIMMING

■ READING TIP:
When you skim a longer reading, don't stop at difficult vocabulary. Skip over it and focus on the ideas you understand.

Quickly skim the article and find three possible solutions to water shortages.

1. _____

2. _____

3. _____

Work with a partner to compare your answers.

SCANNING FOR SPECIFIC INFORMATION.

A. Read the following questions and quickly check to find the answers. Underline the words in the reading that support your answer.

1. How much of Earth's water is fresh water?

_____

2. Where is most of the fresh water located?

_____

3. What percent of Earth's water is renewable?

   _____

4. Where does renewable water come from?

   _____

5. Where are most of the world's desalination plants located?

   _____

6. What two areas in the world depend on imported water?

   a. _____

   b. _____

7. Why is transporting icebergs to the Middle East not a good idea?

   _____

   _____

8. What does the Central Basin district in California use its waste-water for?

   a. _____

   b. _____

   c. _____

9. How much water does the district recycle daily?

   _____

B. Circle the correct choice in each sentence. Then, scan the reading to check your answers. Underline the sentence that contains the correct answer.

1. Salt water is fit/unfit to drink.

2. Most sources of groundwater are renewable/nonrenewable.

3. The high cost of desalination makes it feasible/unfeasible for many developing countries.

4. Solar power is feasible/unfeasible in many water-scarce countries.

5. Many proposals for transporting water are affordable/unaffordable.

6. California uses wastewater for drinking/non-drinking purposes.

7. Something must be done to encourage/discourage greater water conservation.

Work with a partner to compare your answers.

NOTE-TAKING: ADVANTAGES AND DISADVANTAGES

This reading analyzes the advantages and difficulties of different solutions to the problems of water supply. Noting the facts of these ideas helps you to become a critical reader. List three different solutions and the advantages and disadvantages of each in note form.

	Solution	*Advantage*	*Disadvantage*
1.	_____	_____	_____
	_____	_____	_____
	_____	_____	_____
	_____	_____	_____
2.	_____	_____	_____
	_____	_____	_____
	_____	_____	_____
	_____	_____	_____
3.	_____	_____	_____
	_____	_____	_____
	_____	_____	_____
	_____	_____	_____

Work with a partner. Take turns explaining the information about each of the solutions to each other.

After Reading

AGREE OR DISAGREE

Circle A if you agree or D if you disagree with the following statements. Compare your ideas with a partner. Be ready to explain the reasons for your choices.

1. A D   Water should be shared among all countries.

2. A D   We must reduce the amount of water we waste.

3. A D   In the future water will be more expensive.

4. A D   In the future we will have to recycle water more than we do now.

5. A D   We will need to find new sources of water in the future.

6. A D   We will need to develop new technology to keep water clean.

Report on one of the statements you could agree on to the class.

APPLYING THE INFORMATION: IDENTIFYING A PLAN

In the first reading of this chapter, there are some suggestions for ways to save water. Quickly read the short article that follows and identify the type of water saving plan that is explained.

Circle the correct answer.

This article is about

A. A plan to transport water

B. A plan to desalinate water

C. A plan to recycle wastewater

■■
_____

The Living Machine

Dr. Jack Todd is a Canadian marine biologist who is very interested in clean water. He is also interested in saving money, so it's only natural that he is the developer of a small and affordable system to clean wastewater on a very local scale. His "Living Machines" can clean wastewater in your home or in your business.

The "Living Machine" is a system for cleaning wastewater that comes from toilets, baths, dishwashers, washing machines, and any other home plumbing system. The wastewater goes into a big plastic tank where bacteria start to break down the waste. Then, a few days later after it's processed, the water is brought into a greenhouse filled with plants, fish, and algae who feed on it. With the help of sunlight, the plants and animals remove more chemicals from the water, making it cleaner. Then the water can be reused for washing, flushing toilets, or bathing. It cannot be used for drinking or cooking, but the water is clean enough for watering the lawn, washing the dog, or even for bathing or swimming.

The advantage of this technology is that it is affordable and good for the environment. It costs the same as a commercial septic system. The local government saves tax money it would spend to transport waste to large recycling plants. It is good for the environment because wastewater is not put into the fresh-water supply system. If enough homes and businesses used "Living Machines," it could help to reduce the amount of fresh water we need to take from lakes and rivers and it will help keep the water supply unpolluted.

_____

UNDERSTANDING DETAILS IN AN EXTENDED EXAMPLE

The preceding reading describes and explains one way to conserve water. It is an "extended" example, in other words, there is a lot of detail about this system. Answer the following questions that focus on the details of this example.

1. What did Jack Todd develop?

   _____

2. What kinds of wastewater can his system clean?

   _____

3. Where is the wastewater cleaned?

   a. _____

   b. _____

4. How are chemicals removed from the water?

   _____

5. a. What can the water be reused for?

   _____

   _____

   b. What can't the water be reused for?

   _____

   _____

6. What facts show that the system is affordable?

   _____

   _____

7. What facts show that the system is good for the environment?

   _____

Compare answers with your partner. Try to agree on the same answer. Check the reading to confirm your answers.

Vocabulary Building

VOCABULARY IN CONTEXT

You can understand the meaning of a new word by using the words you know to help you make a good guess. Circle the words that help you to guess the meaning of the word in boldface. Write your definition of the word. Then consult a dictionary to check your definition.

1. Because the water was **unfit** to drink, they had to bring in bottled water from the next town. _____

2. They couldn't use the water, because it was **locked up** in the form of glaciers. _____

3. The water is non-renewable, a **finite** resource like oil that is gone forever once it is used. _____

4. Not all countries can get water from **desalination,** because many don't have access to seawater. _____

5. Some needy regions don't have enough water and **rely** on water imports. _____

6. Malta's highly developed tourist trade generates enough **revenue** to pay for water and food. _____

7. The problem is you would have to **stock** the water somewhere for it to be used. _____

8. They use the recycled water for a number of non-drinking uses like the **irrigation** of parks. _____

Work with a partner and take turns reading your sentences and giving your definitions.

SYNONYMS

Match the words in Column A with words that have the same meaning in Column B.

Column A   **Column B**

_____ 1. access   a. produce

_____ 2. agriculture   b. disadvantage

_____ 3. drawback   c. huge

_____ 4. import   d. needed

_____ 5. mammoth   e. fill up again

_____ 6. manufacture   f. not usable

_____ 7. proposal   g. farming

_____ 8. replenish   h. plan

_____ 9. required   i. bring into the country

_____ 10. unfit   j. opening

WORD FORMS

In English, one of the ways the form of a word can be changed is to add a special suffix, or word ending, to change a verb into a noun. In the following sentences the suffix *-tion, -ion,* or *-sion* can be added to a verb root to form nouns.

Choose the correct word to complete the sentences.

1. conserve / conservation

   a. It's important to _____ water for future generations.

   b. The _____ of the country's water supply is important to all of us.

2. solve / solution

   a. They needed to _____ the problems of water supply.

b. They needed to find a _____ to the problems of water supply.

3. pollute / pollution

a. Scientists thought that chemical _____ was causing the damage.

b. If the chemicals _____ the water, the fish may be harmed.

4. desalinate / desalination

a. They are convinced it's important to _____ the seawater.

b. They are convinced that the _____ of the seawater is important.

5. reduce / reduction

a. They decided to _____ the amount of water they were using.

b. We asked them to make a _____ in the amount of water they use.

6. irrigate / irrigation

a. The local government wants to use recycled water to

_____ the parks and golf courses.

b. The local government wants to use recycled water for the

_____ of parks and golf courses.

Check your answers. Work with a partner and take turns reading your sentences.

WORDS WITH THE PREFIX RE-

In English some word prefixes have usual meanings. The prefix *re-* usually means "again," as in the word "renew," or "make it new again."

Give your own definition of the following words. Look at the way the word is used in the reading before you write your definition.

1. renewable _____

2. replenish _____

3. remove _____

4. recycle _____

Expanding Your Language

SPEAKING

A. Oral Presentation. Choose an area of the world and talk about the water resources in that area. Include facts that describe where the water supply comes from, how it is used, what it is used for, and future water problems and possible solutions. Give as many examples as possible.

B. Discussion. Form a group with some classmates who are from different countries. Write three questions to find out about the problems and solutions of water supply. Use your questions to have a discussion about water supply in different parts of the world.

WRITING

A. Topic Writing. Write about the problem of water supply and some possible solutions to this problem. Use the information from the chapter reading. Use examples to help you explain your ideas.

B. Reaction Writing. What can governments and citizens do to save water? Write some details about the suggestions you would make. For example, explain what decisions or plans the government should make, how they would work, who would be involved, and how they would be paid for.

Read On: Taking It Further

READING JOURNAL

■ *READING TIP:*
Don't forget to write your reading journal and vocabulary log entries in your notebook.

There are some very interesting stories that have been written about wild animals and people's relationships with wild animals. One of these stories is *The Call of the Wild*, by the American writer Jack London. You can find this and other stories in condensed or adapted versions. With your teacher's guidance, choose this or another story selection to read and report on.

NEWSPAPER ARTICLES

Check the paper over a few days and find an interesting article about some aspect of the environment. You could look for an article about animals, forests, or parks, or about an issue like water, land, or air conservation. Prepare to present the information to a partner or a small group.

To prepare, follow these steps:

1. Skimming: Quickly read the article to get the general idea and to check if the information is interesting.
2. Ask these questions: What are the facts? Who is involved? When? Where? Why? and How?
3. Highlight the important facts. Make notes if it will help you to explain more easily.
4. Practice your presentation.
5. Present your information.

WORD PLAY

Choose ten new words that you would like to learn from the readings in the unit. Try to choose words that are important, such as nouns, adjectives, adverbs, or verbs. Write a sentence using one of the words. Make your own definition of the word. Find a word or word that has the same meaning. Check the work with your teacher.

Work with a partner. Tell your partner the definition and the synonym and ask your partner to guess the word. Give one letter of the word's spelling until your partner makes a correct guess.

UNIT 5

Personality

A Person Is as Happy as He Makes Up His Mind to Be

—ABRAHAM LINCOLN

Introducing the Topics

In this unit you will read about different aspects of human personality. Each of us has our own unique personality. What we call "personality" is the combination of so many different traits; some we are born with and some develop out of life experience What are some of the ways that we look at an individual's personality? Chapter 13 is about the topic of friendship. How do friendships affect our lives? Chapter 14 explores the feelings of shyness and worry. How do these emotions influence our lives? In Chapter 15 you will discover what some people say our handwriting reveals about our personalities.

Points of Interest

DESCRIBING EMOTIONS

A. Look at the following illustration and circle the faces that show how you are feeling right now.

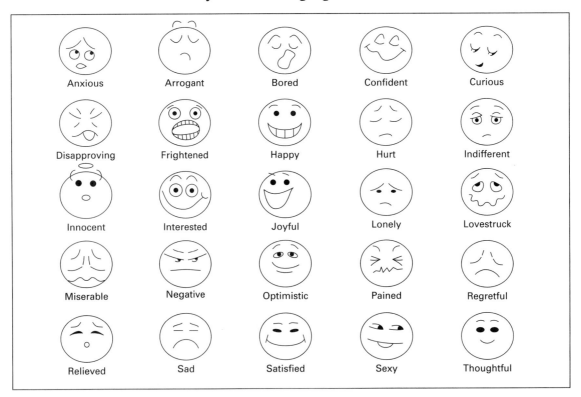

B. Put a check next to the following:

1. Three negative emotions
2. Three positive emotions
3. Three emotions that describe your own personality

Discuss your ideas with a partner or with a small group.

DISCUSSION QUESTIONS

Think about the following questions. Share your ideas with a partner or with a small group. Explain your ideas as completely as possible.

1. What is your definition of "personality"?
2. Does an individual's personality change? If so, how and why does it change?
3. What are a few ways that we can find out what someone's personality is like (for example: daily life experiences, personality tests, etc.)?
4. Does our personality influence our lives? How does this happen?

CHAPTER 3

The Importance
of Friendship

Chapter Openers

Circle A if you agree or D if you disagree with the statement.

1. A   D   People of different ages or different backgrounds can never be friends.

2. A   D   It takes a long time to know if someone is your friend.

3. A   D   We can have friends with very different personalities.

4. A   D   Friends have little influence on our lives.

Work with a partner or a small group. Compare your ideas. Explain your ideas with reasons and examples.

EXPRESSIONS

Here are some expressions about friends and friendship. Discuss what each means with a partner or with a small group. Try to agree on a meaning.

1. A friend in need is a friend indeed.
2. Friends do not lose their flavor.
3. Friendship—one heart in two bodies.

4. Your greatest security lies in your friendships.

5. There is no greater enemy than a false friend.

What sayings about friends do you know? Think of one to share with your classmates.

■ Exploring and Understanding Reading

PREDICTING

■ *READING TIP:*
What reading strategies help you to understand ideas without needing to know all the vocabulary? Keep them in mind as you begin this chapter reading.

This reading is from a weekly newsmagazine that gives information about important people and ideas as well as important news of the week. What kind of information do you expect to find in a weekly newsmagazine article about people's lives? In the following list, check (✔) the item(s) you expect to find.

_____Who is involved in the story.

_____Where and when the story took place.

_____Long explanations about what happened in the story.

_____Short explanations about what happened in the story.

_____Reasons why the story is important.

Compare choices with a partner.

PREVIEWING

Look at the picture, title, and subtitle of this article. Using your predictions and your previewing, make a list of four ideas you expect to find in the reading.

1. _____

2. _____

3. _____

4. _____

Share your ideas with a partner or with a small group.

With a Little Help from Her Friends

Soo Yeun Kim and the students of Jericho High School

Soo Yeun Kim was the kind of student who shows up in the "most likely to succeed" category in high school yearbooks. At Jericho High School in Jericho, N.Y., the 17-year-old was an accomplished flutist, editor of the literary magazine, and a star science student. The week after Thanksgiving, as she was putting the finishing touches on her project for the prestigious Westinghouse Science Talent Search, she and her close friend Joseph Ching were killed in a car accident on a rain-soaked road just a mile from her home.

Jericho had lost two of its best and brightest students—and their grieving friends refused to let Soo Yeun's hard work go to waste. With only two days before the deadline, a group of her classmates joined together to finish her Westinghouse application, some putting off their own work to finish their friend's. Most of her project, a two-year study of bone fragments as they related to the behavior of the Neanderthal man, was already complete. But an eight-page entry form remained, and there were questions that needed answers. What awards had she won? What clubs did she belong to? One question, especially, brought tears to the eyes of her friends: "What would you really like to be doing 10 or 15 years from now?"

The group finished the project in time and, with the help of Soo Yeun's science teacher, Allen Sachs (at left in beard and tie), sent it off to Westinghouse with a note explaining what had been done. But the note was torn off, and judges had no inkling of the circumstances surrounding Soo Yeun's application. Two months later, her project was selected as one of 40 finalists from more than 1,600 applicants. (Since finalists must be interviewed, Soo Yeun's project could go no further.) It was the first time in the competition's 54-year history that Westinghouse has made an award posthumously—a tribute not only to Soo Yeun Kim's hard work but to her selfless friends as well.

SKIMMING

A. Read the complete article quickly and add to or change your prediction statements.

B. Reread the article and answer the following question.

What did Soo Yeun's friends do for her?

_____

CHRONOLOGY: FOLLOWING THE STORY

Read the following statements. Number each according to their order in the story.

_____ a. Soo Yeun and her close friend were killed in a car accident.

_____ b. Westinghouse gave an award to Soo Yeun.

_____ c. Soo Yeun had worked for two years on a project for the Westinghouse Science Talent Search.

_____ d. Soo Yeun was a star science student.

_____ e. Soo Yeun's friends sent her application along with a note.

_____ f. Soo Yeun's project was selected by the judges.

_____ g. Soo Yeun's friends and teacher filled out her application.

_____ h. A group of Soo Yeun's friends decided to finish her application.

Work with a partner to compare the order of the sentences. Locate and underline the information in the article that matches the statements.

UNDERSTANDING DESCRIPTIVE DETAILS

Answer these questions. Underline the details in the reading that support your answer.

1. How did people describe Soo Yeun?

   _____

   _____

2. How did the writer describe Joseph Ching?

   _____

   _____

3. What was Soo Yeun's project?

   _____

   _____

4. What questions were on the application?

   _____

   _____

5. What happened to the note that was sent?

   _____

   _____

6. How are Soo Yeun's friends described?

   _____

   _____

Work with a partner to ask and answer the questions. Look back at the article to compare the information you underlined.

After Reading

REACTING TO THE STORY

Keeping in mind the information in the story and your own experiences, share your ideas about these questions.

1. What does this story tell us about the power of friendship?
2. What is the negative side of this story? What is positive about it?
3. Why does the writer call Soo Yeun's friends "selfless"? Do you know of any other examples of selfless friendship?

APPLYING THE INFORMATION: SIMILARITIES AND DIFFERENCES

Read the following newspaper article. Answer these questions:

1. Did Carol Fleck have selfless reasons to help Ken Purves?
2. Did he accept her offer immediately? Why or why not?
3. How did their friendship develop?
4. What is the negative side of this story? What is the positive side?

■ ■   *New Kidney Is Gift from the Heart*   ■ ■

KELOWNA, B.C. Being a perfect match has taken on a whole new meaning to a Kelowna couple married over the weekend. Just a few weeks after their trip down the aisle, Carol Fleck, 48, and Ken Purves, 53, will make a trip into the operating room where Fleck will donate one of her kidneys to her new husband.

"I'll be fine with one kidney," Fleck says. "And I couldn't be giving a kidney up for a man any more full of integrity and character than Ken."

But Fleck didn't decide to give up one of her organs because she was in love. Love actually came later in the equation. The pair had been casual friends at church. When she learned Purves needed a kidney transplant, Fleck decided she would donate one of her healthy organs if she was a match. He was totally surprised by the offer.

"I didn't know how to respond," said Purves, who's been a widower for four years. "I'd been sick for a long time and I'd been on the donor list for more than 18 months, so I really wasn't talking about it. After all, you really can't go shopping for a kidney."

He eventually accepted Fleck's offer. But she still needed to be tested to see if she was a match.

"I had the tests done, and it takes six weeks to get the results back," said Fleck, a divorcee of eight years. "Ken and I started spending more time together during that six weeks, and the sparks were beginning to fly. By the time we got the results that I'd be a good match on December 17, the romance was well under way."

On Valentine's Day, Purves asked Fleck to marry him. "I didn't mean for us to get married until after the transplant and we were both healthy," he said. "But Carol suggested we get married before so we could go through it as a married couple."

Their involvement with one another can only help: doctors say transplants work better when there's an emotional attachment between donor and recipient.

After the April 27 operation the couple will recover together at a Vancouver hospital.

How do the negative points and positive points of these two stories compare?

Vocabulary Building

VOCABULARY IN CONTEXT

Circle the phrase that is closest in meaning to the words in bold-face in these sentences. Underline the words in the reading that support your answer.

1. Her grieving friends refused to let Soo Yeun's hard work **go to waste**.
   a. be thrown out   b. be lost   c. be used up

2. One question **brought tears to their eyes.**
   a. made them sad   b. bothered their eyes   c. made them angry

3. The note was **torn off** and they didn't know about the circumstances.
   a. cut into many pieces b. returned   c. removed

4. They **sent it off** with a note to explain what they had done.
   a. mailed it   b. exploded it   c. finished it

5. They **had no inkling** of what had happened.
   a. didn't understand   b. didn't write   c. didn't know

6. Carol and Ken will **take a trip down the aisle** together.
   a. take a vacation   b. go shopping   c. get married

Check your answers with a partner.

WORD FORMS

In English many nouns and adjectives come from a verb "root." For example, the noun *decision* and the adjective *decisive* come from the verb root *decide*.

A. Here is a list of verbs. Some of them are "roots" for nouns and adjectives. Write the word forms you know. Look in a dictionary to help you find other forms of the words.

Verb	*Noun*	*Adjective*
1. apply	_____	_____
2. finish	_____	_____
3. accomplish	_____	_____
4. award	_____	_____
5. compete	_____	_____
6. operate	_____	_____
7. involve	_____	_____

Compare lists with a partner.

B. Write three sentences using words from the list.

1. _____

_____

2. _____

_____

3. _____

_____

Expanding Your Language

SPEAKING

A. Retelling: Choose one of the stories you read in this chapter. Make notes of important facts. Try to include as many of the descriptive details as possible. Prepare three discussion questions about the story. Work with a partner to tell the story and discuss the questions.

B. Two-Minute Taped Talk: Tell a story about an important friendship in your life. Describe some of the events in your friendship. As an example, refer to the first reading in this chapter, and include important details: who, what, where, when, and why. Make a short outline of your ideas in note form. Put the information in chronological order. Practice your talk a few times before you record.

WRITING

A. Topic Writing: Using the notes you wrote for Speaking, part A, and your discussion with your partner, write about one of the stories you read in this chapter. Write two paragraphs, one about the facts of the story and the other about your reaction to the ideas in the story.

B. Personal Writing: Write about the topic you chose for the Two-Minute Taped Talk or about your own ideas on the topic of friendship.

CHAPTER 14

Living with Our Emotions

Chapter Openers

DISCUSSION QUESTIONS

Think about the following questions. Discuss your ideas with a partner or with a small group.

1. Do you think shyness is positive, negative, or both?
2. How do people become shy? Are we born shy, or does experience cause shyness?
3. Can people overcome shyness?
4. Do you think worrying is positive, negative, or both?
5. What things in a person's life is it reasonable to worry about? What things is it not reasonable to worry about?
6. Can people learn to stop worrying?

PAIRED READINGS

Choose one of the readings. Work with a partner who is reading the same story.

PREVIEWING FOR THE GENERAL TOPIC

Read the title and the first and last sentences of each paragraph. Then circle the best statement of the main topic of this reading:

A. The reasons that some people are shy.

B. The ways to conquer being shy.

C. Our understanding of shyness and how it can affect people's lives.

Compare answers with a partner. Then read the entire story quickly. As you read, look for the main ideas in each paragraph of the reading.

Reading 1: Can Shyness Be Overcome?

A.   Shy people don't enjoy being with others. They feel very uncomfortable or embarrassed in any situation where others will notice or pay attention to them. Some people feel shy occasionally, while others feel shy all the time. Some claim that shyness allows them to look at things more closely and to listen more completely. But, most people would agree that being shy puts people at a disadvantage. Shy people feel uneasy in social situations. They are often too worried about what other people think of them to be relaxed. At work they dread having to speak at meetings or interact with their coworkers. Extremely shy people may even experience feelings of loneliness and depression, since their feelings prevent them from making friends, trying new experiences, and achieving important goals in life.

B.   Important research has shown some of the reasons for shyness. Shyness is, to some extent, genetic. This means that some people, about 15 percent of us, are shy from birth. Even before being born, the hearts of shy children beat much faster than the hearts of other children. As newborns, these babies feel nervous and cry around others. As very young children, they seem afraid of new experiences. They blush and become embarrassed and some even shake with fear when faced with new people and experiences. But that does not mean that all shy babies necessarily become shy adults. Genetic traits can be changed. In fact, most of the children who are born shy lose their shyness over time. Positive experiences help the children to develop their feelings of self-esteem or self-worth. A shy child who is given the chance to develop an ability for music or sports will gain skills and the confidence to overcome shyness. A parent's praise for the child's accomplishments, as well as a tolerance for failure, is important. Unfortunately, however, not all children develop the confidence and experience to overcome their shyness. Some may suffer feelings of nervousness for many years. The good news is that shy adults can learn to overcome their fears.

C.   There are many ways shy adults can gradually gain control of their uncomfortable feelings. First, they can learn ways to introduce themselves and join in a conversation with others. For example, they can learn how to find common ground for conversation by relating shared experiences, or by asking questions to show the speaker they are interested. Second, they can learn how to ask others about themselves. They can have three or four topics of universal interest, such as the weather, work, school, or the daily news, ready to talk about. They can learn some practical speaking techniques. One technique is to write down the questions you want to ask. Plan what to say, then write the dialogue of what to say and practice the beginning lines. Active listening techniques are useful in overcoming shyness. Learn to listen carefully to what other people say in the course of informal conversation. A good way to do this is to make a mental note of a person's interests as they come up in conversation. A second technique is to listen to the way people begin or end conversations and choose the lines to use in a similar situation. Finally, relaxation techniques, like practicing slow breathing to calm down and thinking about a positive memory, are useful ways to reduce the fear of contact with others. These techniques help a shy person stay calm, look others in the eye, listen, and keep talking.

MAIN IDEAS OF PARAGRAPHS

Write the letter of the paragraph that best fits each of the following main ideas.

1. _____ How adults can overcome shyness.

2. _____ How being shy affects people.

3. _____ Our understanding of the causes of shyness.

Compare answers with a partner.

NOTE-TAKING: RECOGNIZING SUPPORTING POINTS AND DETAILS

Reread the paragraph about the causes of shyness (B) and the paragraph about what to do to overcome shyness (C). Underline the important facts in these paragraphs. From the information you underlined, make notes of the details for each of the sub-points in these paragraphs. Remember to write key words and phrases only. Do not write complete sentences. Be sure you understand the ideas and can explain them to others.

Main Ideas	*Supporting Points/Details*
B. Different causes of shyness	1. Genetic cause of shyness
	2. Influences from experience
C. Useful techniques to overcome shyness in adults	1. Ways to introduce themselves and join in conversation
	2. Techniques for speaking to others
	3. Techniques for listening to others
	4. Relaxation techniques

Work with a partner and take turns comparing the details you wrote. If necessary, look back at the information to add any facts you didn't note or correct any facts you need to.

ANSWERING QUESTIONS FROM NOTES

Use your notes to answer these questions. Circle T for true and F for false.

1. T F   A majority of people are shy from birth.

2. T F   Shy children will remain shy throughout their life.

3. T F   Some experiences help people to gain skills and the confidence to overcome shyness.

4. T F   Shy people can learn to start conversations.

5. T F   Shy people do not need to learn to listen.

6. T F   Relaxation techniques are effective ways to control negative feelings.

READING 2: PREVIEWING FOR THE GENERAL TOPIC

Preview the next selection by reading the title and the first and last sentences of each paragraph. Then circle the best statement of the main topic of this reading:

A. The ways that worry affects people's lives.

B. The ways to cope with worrying.

C. The reasons that people worry.

Compare answers with a partner. Then read the entire selection quickly. As you read, look for the main ideas in each paragraph of the reading.

■ ■

Reading 2: Don't Let Your Worries Get to You

A.   Everyone worries at one time or another. It is a part of our everyday lives. We worry about deadlines, about financial problems, about our relationships with others. Surprisingly, the fact is that worrying is not always a bad thing. Some amount of worry is necessary because it gives us time to concentrate on a problem and find possible solutions or ways to deal with it. Some worry is stimulating. It can propel you to do better work or to complete work on time. When you worry about a problem, you feel uncomfortable. If you don't want to feel uncomfortable, then you will take action to correct the problem. But, in other cases our worries can interfere with our problem-solving abilities. We worry so much that it stops us from taking the steps needed to solve the problem. If it continues, worrying can take away our energy and lead to physical problems such as fatigue, headaches, muscle pain, and insomnia.

B.   If your worries begin to feel overwhelming, don't despair, because there are ways to lower your "worry level." There are two useful techniques to use. One technique is called "progressive relaxation." Lie on the floor or a flat surface such as your bed. Then focus on a specific part of your body, such as your neck and shoulders. Tighten that part of your body. When it feels hard and tense, release the tension and relax. Do this for all the major parts of your body. Continue until you feel totally relaxed. Do this once or twice a day for about ten minutes. When your body is relaxed, it is not as easy to feel worried. The second technique is regular meditation. Sit in a quiet place and close your eyes. Repeat a simple sound that you find pleasing. Repeating a sound helps keep out other thoughts. Do this twice a day for twenty minutes. It helps to relax your mind. When you use these two techniques, you help keep your mind and your body from worrying. In addition to techniques that relieve the body and mind of tension, it is important to develop practical problem-solving techniques to resolve the worries. Worriers often spend a lot of unproductive mental energy thinking "I'll never solve this problem" or "This is just too much for me." Professional counselors or therapists can help worriers to change these negative messages and replace them with more positive thoughts.

C. Unfortunately, for some individuals, worrying is compulsive. In these cases, people find they cannot stop worrying. The reasons for worry are often unlikely events or ideas that are, in some way, irrational. Yet, even this troubling behavior can be modified, especially with professional help. To help someone who worries constantly or in some irrational way, suggest the following steps. First, help the person become aware of worrying thoughts when they first begin. Recognizing the beginning of a worry cycle is very important. The second step is to learn to recognize how one's body feels when the worrying starts. It is important not to allow a repetitive cycle of worry to set in. Instead, as soon as worrying thoughts appear, the person should ask the following questions: What is the possibility of this problem occurring? Could something other than that happen? Could positive actions be taken if the problem occurs? Most people do not experience these kinds of worries. But when continual worrying becomes a problem, it is good to have some strategies for coping.

_____

MAIN IDEAS OF PARAGRAPHS

Write the letter of the paragraph that best fits each of the following main ideas.

1. _____ Techniques for coping with compulsive worrying.

2. _____ How worrying affects us.

3. _____ Some techniques for managing our everyday worries.

Compare answers with a partner.

NOTE-TAKING: RECOGNIZING SUPPORTING POINTS AND DETAILS

■ *READING TIP:*
Analyzing information to see the differences between general (sub-points) and other information (the details) is an important critical reading skill.

Reread the paragraph about how worrying affects us (A) and the paragraph about ways to cope with everyday worries (B). Underline the important facts in these paragraphs. From the information you underlined, make notes of the details for each of the subpoints in these paragraphs. Remember to write key words and phrases only. Do not write complete sentences. Be sure you understand the ideas and can explain them to others.

Main Ideas	*Supporting Points/Details*
How worry affects us	1. Everyday worries
	2. Benefits of worrying
	3. Problems with worrying
Techniques to cope with everyday worries:	1. Problem Solving
	2. Technique 1
	3. Technique 2

Work with a partner and take turns comparing the details you wrote. If necessary, look back at the information to add any facts you didn't note or correct any facts you need to.

ANSWERING QUESTIONS FROM NOTES

Use your notes to answer these questions. Circle T for true or F for false.

1. T F Worrying can be beneficial.

2. T F Worries can keep us from solving problems effectively.

3. T F Worrying affects our mind but not our body.

4. T F Meditation helps the body to relax.

5. T F Problem-solving techniques can be learned.

After Reading

INTERVIEWING

Answer the questionnaire on the topic you read about. Add questions based on the reading or on your own ideas. Interview two people who read the same information. Write their answers in note form on a separate page.

QUESTIONNAIRE: SHYNESS

You:_____   Student A:_____   Student B:_____

1. Do you think you are a shy person?
    a. Yes.   b. No.   c. Sometimes.

2. If you answered no, have you ever felt shy in the past?

3. What experiences do people feel shy about?
    a. Talking to someone you like.
    b. Talking to someone you want to like you.
    c. Talking to someone older than you.
    d. Talking to a person of the opposite sex.
    e. Talking to a member of your family.
    f. Talking to authorities (teachers, bosses, doctors, etc.).
    g. Meeting people one-to-one.
    h. Meeting people in a group.

4. Check the ways to overcome shyness you think are effective.
    a. Try to speak to someone every day.
    b. Join an activity you like.
    c. Listen to how others begin conversations.
    d. Practice having a conversation.
    e. Talk to a counselor about your problems.

QUESTIONNAIRE: WORRY

You:_____   Student A:_____   Student B:_____

1. How often do you worry?
    a. Always.   b. Sometimes.   c. Seldom.

2. What do you usually worry about?
    a. Everyday problems.
    b. Things that are likely to happen.
    c. Things that are unlikely to happen.
    d. Big decisions that have to be made.
    e. Small decisions that have to be made.

3. When you are worried, what do you do?
    a. Think about possible solutions.
    b. Think about the negative things that will happen.
    c. Think about how my worries will affect other people.
    d. Ask for advice from friends and family.
    e. Ask for expert advice from a counselor or other advisor.

MAKING A CHART TO SHOW RESULTS

Work with a partner or with others who answered the same questionnaire as you. Make a list of the results from all the questionnaires in the following chart in note form. Try to summarize the results for your report. For example, you can note the total number who responded yes, who responded no, or who gave similar answers to a question.

Title of Questionnaire: _____			
Question 1	Question 2	Question 3	Question 4

RETELLING THE INFORMATION

■ TIP:
You can begin by asking your partner to answer the questionnaire about your topic before presenting your information.

Work with a partner who read a different selection. Use your notes and the results of your questionnaire to explain the information to your partner.

REACTING TO THE READING

Using the ideas in the two readings, answer these questions.

1. Do shyness and worrying have similar or different effects on personality?
2. Are the strategies for reducing these problems similar or different?
3. Which problem do you think is more common or more serious? Explain.
4. Do you know any reasons for these problems that are not mentioned in the readings?
5. What other solutions for these problems do you know of?

Vocabulary Building

ADJECTIVES TO NOUNS

In English, the form of the word can change when it is used as a different part of speech. For example, a suffix (ending) can be added to change the adjective happy to the noun *happiness*. Some common noun suffixes include -*ness, -ment,* and -*tion*.

Choose the correct form of the word for each of the following sentences. In the parentheses ( ), write which part of speech, noun (n.) or adjective (adj.), is needed to complete the sentence.

1. shy / shyness

    a. People are often _____ (   ) when they meet people for the first time.

    b. Researchers think that _____ (   ) affects a great number of people.

2. relaxed / relaxation

    a. She didn't want to go because she wouldn't feel

       _____ (   ) talking to so many people.

    b. She decided to go home for a night of (   )

       _____ .

3. perfect / perfection

    a. Shy people think that they have to be _____ (   ) when they undertake any new project.

    b. It was clear that she expected nothing but

       _____ (   ) from herself.

4. nervousness / nervous

    a. She kept asking me, "Why do I feel so _____ (   )?"

    b. Her _____ (   ) was very easy to see.

SYNONYMS

Match the words in Column A with the words in Column B that have a similar meaning.

Column A

_____	1. calm
_____	2. productive
_____	3. fatigue
_____	4. contact
_____	5. dread
_____	6. release
_____	7. irrational
_____	8. opportunity
_____	9. notice
_____	10. behavior
_____	11. worry
_____	12. technique
_____	13. traits
_____	14. minimize
_____	15. blush

Column B

a. unreasonable

b. action

c. let go

d. characteristics

e. observe

f. reduce

g. turn red with embarrassment

h. giving good results

i. possibility

j. tiredness

k. procedure

l. meet

m. anxiety

n. relaxed

o. fear

ANTONYMS

The prefix *un-*, meaning "not," added to the beginning of some words to give that word a negative or opposite meaning, for example, *happy* and *unhappy*. Words that are opposite in meaning are called *antonyms*.

Scan the readings and find as many words as you can that begin with the prefix *un-*. Write the word and give its antonym. Use the word in a sentence of your own.

Word	Antonym	Sentence
_____	_____	_____
_____	_____	_____
_____	_____	_____
_____	_____	_____
_____	_____	_____
_____	_____	_____

Here are some other negative prefixes:

il-, as in *legal, illegal*

in-, as in *adequate, inadequate*

im-, as in *possible, impossible*

Write a short list of words you know that have antonyms that begin with a negative prefix.

_____	_____
_____	_____
_____	_____

Check your list with your teacher.

Expanding Your Language

SPEAKING

Two-Minute Taped Talk: Use the notes and ideas you prepared for the paired reading. Organize your notes to prepare a two-minute talk on the parts of the information you think are important. You can choose to present the information you heard about from your partner, or you can combine parts of both articles in your talk. Make an outline of your ideas in note form. Practice your talk a few times before you record. Try to explain as clearly and naturally as possible.

WRITING

Topic Writing: Based on your notes for the paired reading and your discussion with your partner, write about the information you read. In separate paragraphs write about the facts and your reaction to the ideas in the reading.

Handwriting and Our Personality

Chapter Openers

DISCUSSION QUESTIONS

Think about the following questions. Share your ideas with a partner or with a small group.

In signing a passport or a personal letter, we write our signature. Write your signature on the following line:

_____

1. Is your signature easy or difficult to read?
2. Do you usually sign your signature the same way?
3. Has your signature changed over time? How?
4. How do you feel about your handwriting?
5. Do you find it easy or difficult to read other people's handwriting?
6. What can we learn about people's personalities from analyzing their handwriting?

INFO-GAP: GETTING INFORMATION FROM DIAGRAMS

Complete either Set A or Set B. Circle your answer.

SET A

1. Who is moodier, A or B?

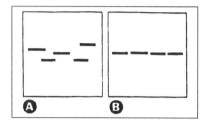

2. Who likes to be in the middle of everything?

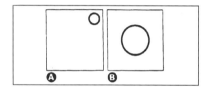

3. Who is lying about his or her age?

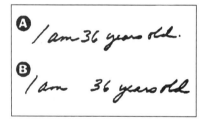

4. Which "Jack" is going to get a raise in his salary?

Figure A

Please have Jack come see me

Figure B

Please have Jack come see me

Discuss your answers with a partner. Check the answer key.

SET B

5. Who has a higher IQ?

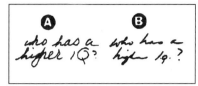

6. Which person is dishonest about money?

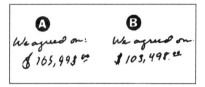

7. Which "Mrs. Smith" wants a divorce from "Mr. Smith"?

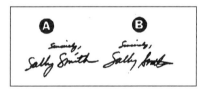

8. Which one of these two writers is more likely to break the law?

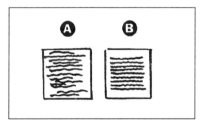

Discuss your answers with a partner. Check the answer key. Work with a person who has worked on a different set of diagrams. Ask your partner to answer your set of questions. Discuss the reasons for your choices before giving the answers.

Exploring and Understanding Reading

PREDICTING

This reading is on the topic of graphology, the analysis of handwriting. What ideas do you expect the reading to contain? Check the items you expect to find in the following list.

_____   Origin of handwriting analysis

_____   What handwriting analysis can't tell you

_____   How handwriting analysis works

_____   How handwriting analysis is used

_____   Who doesn't use handwriting analysis

Compare answers with a partner.

SKIMMING

■ *READING TIP:*
Remember to read quickly when you skim. Don't let yourself stop to think about each word individually or about any one word that you may not understand immediately.

Skim the reading and check any of the predictions in the preceding list that you found there. Write two main ideas that you remember from the reading. Share your ideas with a partner. Make a list of common ideas with your classmates.

1. _____

2. _____

Graphology: Can It Be Trusted?

A. Graphology is more than just the study of handwriting. It is the study of all forms of graphic movement, including drawing and doodling. In the United States, graphology has not been considered a legitimate science, but it is studied seriously in Europe, where it developed in the early twentieth century along with the science of psychiatry. Psychiatrists such as Freud and Jung thought this analysis was a very useful tool for understanding both the conscious and the unconscious workings of the mind. For them, handwriting was like a window into the brain. They could look into a person's personality by examining certain movements of the pen, or the way the size or style of the handwriting changed, or if an unusual amount of space was left between words in a sentence. From a writing sample, graphologists claim they can find out the following things about a person:

Country/region of origin
Level of intelligence
Emotional stability
Aptitudes and talents
Leadership qualities
Honesty level
Physical activity level
Work/school performance
Alcoholism or drug abuse

B. In general, graphologists use five different tools in analyzing written or graphic work. These are:

1. *Physical signs:* When a writer's hand shakes, the writing will shake. When a writer is tense and nervous, the person will push harder on the page. These signs could indicate illness, dishonesty, or drug or alcohol abuse. Or it might be that the person is trying to hide his or her true identity.

2. *Psychological signs:* A graphologist has to understand basic psychological theory. For example, one of Freud's ideas was that if a person overdid something, it meant that the opposite was true. If the word *LOVE* in the sentence "I love you" was written in letters very much larger than the rest, the graphologist would know that, according to Freud's theory, it could mean that the writer does not feel love.

3. *Universal concepts:* According to anthropologist Desmond Morris, there are certain universal body movements showing emotions such as sadness, love, pain, and anger. Since handwriting is one of our body movements, we can assume a link between a movement and an emotion. For example, a person who writes with an upward motion feels happy and a person who writes big feels important.

4. *Commonsense signs:* A person who is neat and tidy will write in an orderly way. People who are messy or don't like their name will not write their signature clearly.

5. *Scientific method:* A lot of research involves the study of large numbers of handwriting samples. Graphologists get writing samples from special groups of people. Then they compare these samples to the handwriting of the general population. For example, in one study, criminals serving time in prison were asked to write on a blank page. Researchers found that many did not begin their sentences at the left-hand margin, a general rule of writing that is learned in school. Through research, graphology has identified twenty-five different handwriting traits that are more common among criminals than in others.

C. Can graphology be trusted to give reliable results? The answer is not clear. But there is growing interest in graphology in the United States. Businesses are beginning to look at handwriting analysis as a way to find the right employee. It is expensive to hire workers, train them, and then six months later find that they are not right for the job. The head of a car dealership is one example of some 6,000 business executives who admit using handwriting analysis to help hire the right people. Tom Payette's car dealership is worth $25 million. With handwriting analysis, he has reduced the rate of employees who leave the job to half of the national average. He also uses handwriting analysis to help decide promotions and other job changes. The results are not 100 percent accurate. But, if it saves thousands of dollars in lost time and training, then executives like Tom Payette say it is worth it.

SCANNING FOR DETAILS

A. Complete the following sentences.

1. Graphology is the study of _____.

   _____.

2. In the United States, graphology has not been considered a

   _____, but it is studied

   _____ in Europe.

3. Freud and Jung used graphology to study both the

   _____ and the _____ mind.

4. Graphologists use _____ _____ _____
   in analyzing written or graphic work.

B. Answer the following questions. Underline the information that supports your answer.

1. What kind of information can a graphologist find from looking at a person's writing?

   _____

   _____

2. What three characteristics of handwriting did psychiatrists look at to understand personality?

   _____

3. a. What are the five different types of diagnostic tools a graphologist uses?

   b. How is each tool used? What information can you get from using this tool?

Now write the information in the following chart.

	Type of tool	*How it works*	*Information it provides*
a.			
b.			
c.			
d.			
e.			

4. a. What are businesses interested in using handwriting analysis for?

   _____

   _____

   b. Why is handwriting analysis interesting for businesses?

   _____

   _____

Work with a partner to compare your answers.

After Reading

APPLYING THE INFORMATION

The following is an excerpt from an interview with graphologist Andrea McNicol. Andrea studied graphology at the University of Heidelberg and the Sorbonne. She teaches a course on the subject at the University of California, and she has given expert testimony in several court cases involving handwriting analysis. She is explaining to the interviewer how she used her skills in handwriting analysis to help solve a crime in which money was stolen from a company by an employee. From the information you have gathered so far, do you think she will show that handwriting analysis:

a. can solve a crime directly?

b. can solve a crime indirectly?

c. cannot solve a crime at all?

Discuss your prediction with a partner. Read the selection as quickly as possible to see if your prediction is correct.

■ ■

The Lowdown on Handwriting Analysis

I've had people make some concerted attempts to mask their writing, but it virtually never works. A lie can be identified on the page. See for yourself. Take a look at the two paragraphs:

Cashier A

I stocked the frozen food section between 4 & 5 a.m. I cashed out registers 3 4 and 5 before leaving and put approximately $2700 into the deposit slot in the safe. I left at 6.

Janitor

And there was a pill in the dairy ile which I cleaned up. I put away the cart and put the trash in the back, and then I left work at my usual time of 6:00 in the morning.

Andrea: I investigated a case a few years ago involving a theft of $52,000 from the vault of a department store. The theft occurred sometime between 10 P.M. and 6 A.M. Assuming that it was an inside job, since there were no signs of forced entry, the owners asked the two workers on duty that night to write down what their activities were. What stands out in these two letters?

Int: "The Cashier's writing seems strained . . . and the slant is a little inconsistent. The janitor has a variety of slants, too, yet his letter seems less stressed."

Andrea: You're right about the slants. Cashier A may have a tendency to repress, but that doesn't necessarily mean criminal intent. A good first step in interpreting a page is to examine the spacing. If there are exaggerated spaces between words, the writer's mind was pausing or hesitating while writing them. Why were they hesitating? You've got to make an *effort* to lie on the page, an effort that interrupts the normal flow of your writing. The truth usually flows pretty easily.

So what can we conclude from the statements? It seems clear that the large spaces in the janitor's letter between the words *at* and *my* as well as between *of* and *6:00* suggest that he did not leave at the time indicated.

I called the manager and said that I could not conclude from the letters who stole the money, but that the janitor was probably lying about the time at which he'd left that night. It turned out that he was told to leave early by the day manager, who had unexpectedly shown up two hours early that morning, but hadn't informed anyone of his arrival. The manager was later identified as the thief.

---

1. Did handwriting analysis produce direct, indirect, or no evidence

   of the crime? ———

2. Would you change your predicted answer? ——— Why?

Work with a partner. Agree on your answers to the following questions. Look back at the reading to confirm your answers.

REACTING TO THE READING: USEFUL OR NOT?

Referring to your readings in this chapter and your own ideas, answer the following questions.

Do you think that handwriting analysis can be useful in helping people make decisions when they are doing the following things?

- Hiring new employees
- Diagnosing emotional problems
- Solving crimes
- Establishing the identity of a person

Vocabulary Building

WORD FORMS

The suffix *-ist* is added to a noun form to indicate a person who is an expert or a student of a particular field of study or who works in that field. One example is the word *biologist,* meaning "a person who studies or works in biology."

A. Scan the reading "Graphology: Can It Be Trusted?" and find examples of nouns ending in *-ist*. Write the noun and give a definition in your own words.

Noun	*Meaning*
_____	_____
_____	_____
_____	_____

B. Write the adjective form of the following words:

Noun   *Adjective*

1. intelligence   _____

2. space   _____

3. emotion   _____

4. psychology   _____

5. psychiatry   _____

6. criminal   _____

7. importance   _____

Which word has the same form as an adjective and as a noun?

_____

ANTONYMS

Use what you know about the prefixes that can mean "not" and scan the readings to find words that have a negative prefix. Write the word and its antonym. Number 1 is given as an example.

1. unconscious   conscious

2. _____   _____

3. _____   _____

4. _____   _____

5. _____   _____

Tell your partner a word, and ask for the correct antonym.

Expanding Your Language

WRITING

A. Free Writing: Write about one or more of the following topics.

- How do you feel about your handwriting? What does it show about your personality?
- How did you develop your handwriting? How has it changed?
- How would you compare your handwriting in your first and second languages?

B. Topic Writing: Write about three or four of the important ideas you learned in the two chapter readings. Explain each idea as completely as possible. Refer to Chapter 1 page 12 for guidelines to follow.

SPEAKING

Oral Presentation: Collect writing samples from two or three people. Based on the information in the readings, analyze the samples. Prepare notes about the findings you made. Present your information to others in a small group. Invite your listeners to ask questions about your analysis.

Read On: Taking It Further

READING JOURNAL: RETELLING

■ *READING TIP:* Don't forget to write your reading journal and add vocabulary log entries to your note-book. Show your entries to your teacher. Arrange to discuss your progress in reading.

There are some interesting stories about people who have overcome difficulty to achieve important goals in their lives. One example is the story of Harriet Tubman, a black woman who brought many people out of slavery in the 1860s. Another example is the story of Christopher Reeve, an actor who is paralyzed as the result of an accident and is determined to walk again. With your teacher's guidance, choose a story to read about and report on.

NEWSPAPER ARTICLES

Check the newspaper or a newsmagazine over a few days and find an interesting article of courage and character like those you read in Chapter 13. Follow the steps for this activity on page 150 in Unit 4.

WORD PLAY: A NEW-FASHIONED SPELLING BEE

Work in small groups of four or more. Form two teams within the group. Each team makes a list of ten to fifteen (or more!) important vocabulary words from any of the chapters in this unit. You can assign certain parts of the alphabet to avoid having words appear on both lists. Teams take turns asking the other team to spell a word on their list. The team to spell the most words correctly wins. You can make the game more difficult by varying the rules. Suggestions include using the word correctly in a sentence, spelling without writing, or spelling within a time limit.

The Search for Answers

The Fairest Thing We Can Experience Is the Mysterious.
—ALBERT EINSTEIN

Introducing the Topics

People are always interested in solving mysteries. Asking questions is an important key to solving mysteries. This unit is about topics that have fascinated and puzzled people for many years. In Chapter 16 you will share in the discovery of the world's oldest completely preserved man and find out what can be learned from studying the Iceman. Chapter 17 examines what happened to the *Titanic* and what plans people have to raise the boat. Chapter 18 is about the Anasazi. What led them to abandon their magnificent homes in the American Southwest?

Points of Interest

FINDING REASONS

A. Write down your thoughts about this question on a separate piece of paper.

What can we learn from studying the past? Find three or more reasons why it is important.

B. Group Work: With your group find the similarities and differences among your ideas. Make a list of three reasons for studying the past that your group can agree on. Present your list to your classmates.

DISCUSSION QUESTIONS

Think about these questions. Share your ideas with a partner or with a small group.

1. What mysterious events have occurred in your lifetime?
2. If you had to solve a mystery, how would you do it?
3. What kind of mysteries would these people solve: doctors, archaeologists, engineers, reporters, police officers? How would they do it?
4. Do you know of any important mysteries people are trying to solve today? Explain.

CHAPTER 16

The Mystery of the Iceman

Chapter Openers

DISCUSSION QUESTIONS

Think about these questions. Share your ideas with a partner or with a small group.

1. What is archaeology?
2. What famous archaeological sites do you know about? Where are they located?
3. Is it important to find out about the lives of prehistoric people? Why? What can we learn from studying them?
4. Can people visit prehistoric sites without destroying them?

Exploring and Understanding Reading

PREDICTING

This reading is about the discovery of a 5,000-year-old man. What important information about this discovery do you think you might learn from this reading? List four ideas.

1. where the body was discovered

2. _____

3. _____

4. _____

5. _____

Share your ideas with a partner or with a small group.

SKIMMING

A. Read the complete story quickly and add to or change your prediction statements.

B. Reread the story and answer the following question: Why was this discovery important?

_____

_____

■ ■

The Iceman of the Alps

On September 19, 1991, Helmut Simon and his wife, Erika, were on a hiking vacation in the Alps between Austria and Italy. They were walking alone, enjoying the views, when they noticed something sticking out of the snow. When they got close, they could see that it was a human head. Helmut noticed what looked like a hole at the back of the head. They wondered if this person could have been murdered. They decided to try to reach a phone and contact the police. The couple stopped at a hiker's shelter and told the owner about their discovery. The owner contacted both the Italian and Austrian police. The Italian police were too busy to investigate right away. The Austrian police were not able to come right away either.

The news of the discovery spread and over the next few days people did come. An Austrian police officer arrived first. He tried to take the body out of the ice with a jackhammer. This powerful machine ripped through the thick ice, but it also damaged part of the body. Fortunately, the jackhammer ran out of power before too much damage was done. Other people who heard about the discovery came and tried unsuccessfully to free the body. Finally, on September 23, Dr. Rainer Henn, a scientist who examines dead bodies, came to investigate. He immediately noticed that the body did not look white and waxy like most bodies do. It looked yellow and dry, like the body of a mummy. He borrowed a pickax and a ski pole and dug the body out.

Dr. Henn suspected that the body was very old. He flew the body by helicopter to Innsbruck, Austria. He wanted to get the body to a laboratory for tests to find out the man's age. In Innsbruck, the body was put in a coffin and kept in a warm room. Photographers and reporters were called in for a press conference. The room got warmer under the camera lights. People were smoking and touching the body. After a few hours, a fungus started growing on the body. Finally, Dr. Konrad Spindler, an archaeologist specializing in prehistoric man, was brought in. He was amazed by what he saw. He knew immediately that this was the body of very ancient man; a man perhaps as much as 4,000 years old. And he also knew that the body would have to be moved to a refrigerated room to prevent further damage. The fungus was growing and the body was in danger. Dr. Spindler put the body into a cold, damp room with 98-percent humidity at minus six degrees Celsius. Here the body was safe for scientists to study.

Archaeologists from around the world wanted to study this Stone Age man. They made a number of exciting discoveries about the Iceman. First, tests showed that the Iceman was between 5,000 and 5,500 years old, making him the oldest completely preserved human being ever found. As they examined the body, archaeologists found some new things that tell us about very old human customs and behaviors. One of the discoveries was that there were strange markings, like tattoos, drawn on the man's back. Someone had made these tattoos. Before the Iceman, no one knew that tattooing was practiced that early. What was the purpose of the tattoos? Were they religious symbols or the mark of a brave leader or hunter? The second interesting discovery was that his clothes were made of leather from the skins of three different animals. He had a cape made from grass. Who could have sewed his clothes? It looked as if someone skilled in sewing had made them. The Iceman's hair was only 9 centimeters long and it was evenly cut. No one ever thought that people had been cutting their hair that long ago. Some mushrooms were found with the body. Were they used for medicine? The Iceman gave archaeologists a much more complete picture of the daily life of ancient people who lived fifty-three centuries ago.

Scientists want to continue studying the Iceman. Some would like to take tiny samples from the body for DNA analysis. This analysis would tell us about the man's genetic makeup and answer some important questions. What diseases had he had? How did he die? How have human genes changed over the centuries? We could even discover who his closest living relatives are. Some politicians in the town near the discovery site want to put the body in a museum for people to see. But scientists are concerned about these plans. They don't want the body to become a tourist attraction. They feel strongly that it should be preserved for science and for future generations to study.

———————

CHRONOLOGY: FOLLOWING THE STORY

Read the following statements. Number them according to their order in the story.

_____ a. The body is brought to Innsbruck.

_____ b. An Austrian police officer tries to remove the body with a jackhammer.

_____ c. Scientists discover the true age of the body.

_____ d. The Iceman and his possessions are studied by archaeologists.

_____ e. Tourist companies invite people to visit the area where the body was discovered.

_____ f. Helmut and Erika Simon see a body in the ice.

_____ g. The body is moved to a refrigerated room to prevent damage.

_____ h. The police are too busy to investigate.

_____ i. Dr. Konrad Spindler identifies the body as that of a prehistoric man.

_____ j. Dr. Henn examines the body.

_____ k. Scientists would like to study the body's DNA structure.

Work with a partner to compare the order of the sentences. Together locate and underline the information in the reading that matches the statements. Take turns reading the sentences aloud in the correct order.

UNDERSTANDING DESCRIPTIVE DETAILS

A. Connecting Words to Pictures: Look carefully at the sentences in the reading that describe what archaeologists found when they examined the Iceman. Use your scanning and guessing strategies to identify what is in this illustration.

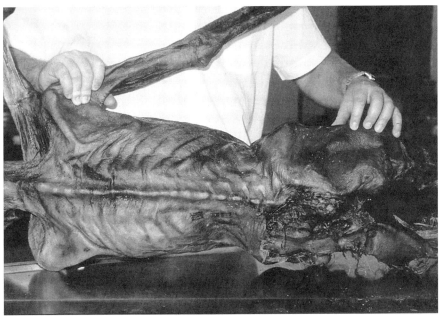

B. Identifying Elements of a Story: An important part of this story is the work of different people to solve the mystery. Match the person or people in Column A to the work they did in Column B.

Column A

_____ 1. Helmut and Erika Simon

_____ 2. Italian police

_____ 3. An Austrian police officer

_____ 4. Dr. Rainer Henn

_____ 5. Dr. Konrad Spindler

_____ 6. Archaeologists

_____ 7. DNA scientists

_____ 8. Politicians

Column B

a. want to find out what diseases he had and how he died.

b. made discoveries about the Iceman's daily life.

c. knew that the body was very old.

d. found the Iceman's body.

e. knew the body did not look like most dead bodies.

f. were too busy to investigate the body.

g. want the Iceman in a museum for tourists to visit.

h. tried to remove the body with a jackhammer.

Work with a partner and take turns reading your sentences. Try to agree on the same answer. Look back at the reading if you disagree.

C. Question Making: Scan the reading and find five questions that archaeologists and others asked about the Iceman. Underline the questions. Compare the questions you underlined with a partner.

After Reading

DEBATING THE ISSUES TODAY

We have a rare opportunity to see and study the body of a person who lived 5,000 years ago. Should the body be available for scientists to study? Should it be put in a museum? What are the benefits of both ideas?

Prepare to debate this question by following these steps:

1. Choose the side you will argue (leave the body for scientists to study or put the body in a museum).
2. Make a list of ideas in support of your position.
3. Work with one or more partners arguing the same position and add to your list of ideas.
4. Practice your oral presentation.
5. Present and argue your position against a person who prepared the other side.
6. Make a list of all the arguments for and against with your classmates. As a class decide what you think should be done.

Vocabulary Building

VOCABULARY IN CONTEXT

Use your understanding of one part of the sentence to help you guess the word that is missing. Your knowledge of English grammar will help you make the right choice.

Complete each sentence with one of the following verbs.

a. borrowed	d. enjoy	g. noticed	i. suspected
b. contacted	e. investigated	h. prevent	j. touched
c. grow	f. move		

1. She _____ when she saw something that looked strange.

2. At first no one _____ that the body was that old.

3. He _____ the police and told them what happened.

4. The body was damaged because so many people had

   _____ it.

5. He _____ a pickax because he didn't have any tools of his own.

6. They _____ the tattoos on his back after they took off his clothes.

7. Some people want to _____ the body, but others want it to stay where it is.

8. She put on a bandage to _____ the cut from getting infected.

9. They wanted to visit the area and just _____ a walk in the mountains.

10. We didn't know that the fungus could _____ and spread so quickly.

Check your answers. Work with a partner and take turns reading your sentences.

JIGSAW SENTENCES

Use your understanding of key words to match each of the sentences in Column A with the sentence in Column B that would best follow it.

Column A

_____ 1. Some mushrooms were found with the body.

_____ 2. He had a cape made from grass.

_____ 3. He carried material for making a fire.

_____ 4. The body had strange markings on its back.

Column B

a. This was the first evidence that tattooing was practiced that long ago.

b. Were they used for medicine?

c. He kept this material in his backpack.

d. The clothes showed that someone skilled in sewing had made the garment.

Work with a partner and take turns reading the sentence pairs. Check your answers.

WORD FORMS

In English we often add the suffix *-er* or *-ist* to the end of a root word to show what a person does. For example, a *teacher* is "a person who teaches," and an *artist* is "a person who creates works of art."

Reread the text and find some examples of words that describe what people do and that end in *-er*, *-ist*, or *-ian*. Write the word and a definition in your own words.

Word	*Definition*
_____	_____
_____	_____
_____	_____
_____	_____
_____	

Expanding Your Language

SPEAKING

Two-Minute Taped Talk: What did you learn about the discovery of the Iceman? Based on your own ideas and the information in this chapter, prepare a two-minute tape to talk about the topic. Prepare your ideas before you record. Make a short outline of your ideas in note form. Practice your talk a few times before you record. Give it to your teacher for feedback on content and clarity of ideas.

WRITING

Topic Writing: Write about the topic of your taped talk. Follow the instructions in Chapter 1, page 12.

CHAPTER 17

What Will Happen to the *Titanic?*

Chapter Openers

DISCUSSION QUESTIONS

Think about these questions. Share your ideas with a partner or with a small group.

1. What do you know about the story of the *Titanic*?
2. Why are people interested in the story of the *Titanic*?
3. What questions have people asked about the *Titanic* over the years?

PAIRED READINGS

Choose one of the readings. Work with a partner who is reading the same story.

SKIMMING

Read quickly and then answer the following questions.

1. Why was this ship so special?

_____

2. What was its fate?

_____

Work with a partner to compare your answers.

■ ■   *Reading 1: The Tragedy of the* **Titanic**   ■ ■

BY ROBERT D. BALLARD

It's Wednesday, April 10, 1912, and hundreds of people are arriving in Southampton, England, for the adventure of a lifetime—the maiden voyage of the R.M.S. *Titanic.*

The ship is unsinkable, a marvel of modern engineering. She's 882 feet long, weighs 42,000 tons, and, if stood on end, would rise higher than the pyramids of Egypt and would tower over the Washington monument.

She's a floating palace. A first-class one-way ticket would cost up to $50,000 today.

So Much to See, So Little Time

Excitement fills the air as the children explore this greatest ship that will carry them across the Atlantic Ocean. So many things to see and all of them brand-new.

The carpets are thick, the linens clean, and the big dining rooms lined with rich wooden paneling. There are even elevators to carry people from deck to deck, down into the bowels of the ship-where the swimming pool and squash court are found.

It's hard to sleep the first night for fear of missing something wonderful. But fatigue overtakes the travelers as the sounds of the band drift off into the dark chilly night.

Each day brings new adventure, but just as it begins to seem the cruise could never end, word comes that the ship is approaching the shore of Canada. New York City is not so far away.

Quick Conferences in the Radio Room

That night, April 14, the older children are allowed to stay up a little longer. Some peek into the windows of the radio operators. There they see the radioman, Jack Phillips, but he is too busy to notice.

Just then another man walks into the radio room. It's hard to hear him talk—but it's something about icebergs. Phillips hands a note to his assistant, Harold Bride, who quickly disappears.

The children want to explore the bridge, but it's getting cold. Time to head off to a warm soft bed.

Iceberg, Dead Ahead!

Huddled in the crow's nest high on the forward main mast is the lookout, Fred Fleet. As he stares out into the dark eternal night he suddenly sees something straight ahead.

"Iceberg: right ahead!" he yells.

He quickly calls the bridge, but there is not much they can do. The ship is traveling too fast. As she turns to port (left) the iceberg passes down the starboard (right) side. Fleet braces for the collision.

But surprisingly it doesn't seem too bad, just a gentle nudge as a few chunks of ice fall onto the deck. The iceberg disappears in the ship's wake as some of the passengers playfully throw bits of the iceberg at each other.

The Ship Is Going to Sink in One Hour

Below decks, it's a different situation. There Captain Edward J. Smith and the *Titanic's* builder, Thomas Andrews, find water pouring into the mail room, the forward holds, and the two boiler rooms.

The hole in the side of the ship doesn't seem to be large. But it's not the size of the hole that seems to be bothering Andrews—it's the length of the damage. The *Titanic* can float if four of her sixteen watertight compartments are flooded. But water is flowing into at least five.

Quickly Andrews completes his mental calculations and turns to Captain Smith. "The ship is gong to sink in an hour to an hour and a half," he reports grimly.

The captain is stunned. He knows that there aren't enough lifeboats for everyone aboard. The ship's owners hadn't thought them necessary.

A Desperate Call for Help

Returning to the bridge, Captain Smith tells the radio operator to send out a series of distress calls. Perhaps there is help nearby. On the horizon to the north he can see the lights of a ship. Maybe the radio operator can raise the crew. Maybe they will see the distress rockets. He orders them shot into the still night.

Initially the lateness of the night, the calmness of the sea, and the ship's soft impact with the iceberg lull the passengers into thinking that nothing is really wrong. They are on the *Titanic*, aren't they? Isn't she unsinkable?

At first the passengers don't want to climb into the lifeboats. They can't even see the surface of the sea far below. Why would anyone want to leave this wonderful ship and venture into a cold, dark world in a tiny boat? It seems so nice on the boat deck where the band is now playing. But the boats are lowered anyway. Many are half empty as they row away toward the light on the distant northern horizon.

Now Only Death Awaits

It is only when the *Titanic* begins to take on a severe downward angle that the passengers begin to realize that only death awaits them.

Panic breaks out as everyone rushes to the stern only to find that there are no more lifeboats left. In desperation they begin jumping into the sea—a sea so cold that they are dead within an hour. The sounds of their screams are mixed with the even louder death groans of the ship.

Then a chilling silence falls across the surface of the sea. What began as the greatest sea voyage of all time has ended in great disaster. Of the more than 2,200 people aboard moments ago, only 705 are saved. The *Titanic* is gone forever,—or is she?

SCANNING FOR DESCRIPTIVE DETAILS

■ READING TIP:
Marking the question number in the margin of a text is another way to locate the information for your answers quickly.

Look back at the reading for the answers to these questions. Mark the question number in the margin of the page. Write your answers in note form.

1. What luxuries did the ship offer its passengers?

    _____

    _____

2. What happened on the night of April 14, 1912?

    _____

    _____

3. What message did the ship's builder give the captain?

    _____

    _____

4. a. What was the captain's reaction?

    _____

    _____

   b. Why did he react this way?

    _____

    _____

   c. What did he give orders to do?

    _____

    _____

5. How did the passengers react to the accident at first?

    _____

    _____

6. When did the passengers start to panic?

    _____

    _____

7. How did the tragedy end?

_____

_____

Work with a partner to ask and answer the questions. Compare the information you marked in the margin.

NOTE-TAKING: CHRONOLOGY OF EVENTS

Scan the reading quickly and find ten to twelve facts about the events that took place aboard the *Titanic* the night of the sinking. Note these facts in the order they occurred.

EVENTS ON THE TITANIC *THE NIGHT OF APRIL 14*

1. radio operator receives message about icebergs/too busy to notice

2. _____

_____

3. _____

_____

4. _____

_____

5. _____

_____

6. _____

_____

7. _____

_____

8. _____

_____

9. _____

_____

10. _____

_____

11. _____

_____

12. _____

_____

RECAPPING THE EVENTS

Work with a partner who took notes about the same story. Take turns explaining several of the facts to each other. As you talk, be sure to explain the events in the order they occurred. Check to make sure that you both have the same information. Add or correct any facts you need to.

SKIMMING

Read the selection on page 212 quickly and then answer the following questions.

1. Why was this search different from others?

_____

2. When did they find the *Titanic*?

_____

Work with a partner to compare your answers.

Reading 2: The **Titanic** *Found!*

BY ROBERT D. BALLARD

When the R.M.S. *Titanic* was lost in 12,500 feet of water in 1912, no one thought that she would ever be found. A series of attempts was made in the 1980s, but all failed to locate the shipwreck.

But during the summer of 1985, my team from the Woods Hole (Massachusetts) Oceanographic Institution found the *Titanic* sitting right-side up on the bottom of the Atlantic Ocean. The world was amazed to hear "The *Titanic* found!"

Why did our search prove successful when others failed?

The answer lay in our key strategy. When the *Titanic* struck an iceberg on April 14, 1912, it opened a wound in the starboard (right) side of the ship. Water rushed into the forward compartments, causing her to sink at the bow.

Slowly her giant stern began to rise into the air, creating stress on the weaker midsection of the ship. Ships of her design had large dining areas and salons in the central part of the ship, rooms that could not support the full weight of the stern. So as her stern rose even higher there was a sudden, tremendous noise and rush of air as the ship split in half.

As the hull began to tear, all sorts of objects poured into the sea. *Titanic's* massive boilers, her safes, cooking pots, dishes, tons of coal, everything imaginable began a free fall to the bottom.

A Mile of Debris

As these objects fell, the ocean current that brought the icebergs from the north swept the objects away. The lighter the object, the farther it was swept. Some items fell through the surface currents in a few minutes. But many objects, like the deck furniture, lingered in the current longer. The lifeboats carrying the survivors drifted for hours.

By the time all the objects had finally come to rest on the bottom, they created a trail of debris more than one mile long.

We looked for the debris trail, not the ship. That's why we were so interested in the log book of the *Californian* the ship the people on the *Titanic* had seen that night drifting on the northern horizon. The *Californian* shut down her engines that night to avoid the icebergs, but her logbook would show valuable information about the currents that caused the ship to drift to the south. Once we knew about these currents, we could set our search strategy.

Up and Back, Up and Back

We began in the area where the *Carpathia*, the first rescue ship to arrive, had picked up *Titanic's* lifeboats. We knew the *Titanic's* hull could *not* be south of this location.

Once there, we lowered our towed camera system, *Argo*, more than two miles to just above the bottom of the ocean and began a series of long search lines running east to west, perpendicular to the trail of debris we were looking for.

As we completed our westerly line, we turned north for one mile before turning back to the east to begin another long search line.

Slowly we progressed toward the *Californian's* position. Then, on September 1, 1985, *Argo's* sensitive cameras passed over the trail of debris we were looking for.

At first, we saw small, light objects, but as we continued, the objects that we saw were heavier and heavier, until suddenly one of the *Titanic's* massive boilers passed under *Argo*. Then we saw the ship's gigantic stern.

The *Titanic* was finally found!

SCANNING FOR DESCRIPTIVE DETAILS

Look back at the reading for the answers to these questions. Mark the question number in the margin of the page. Write your answers in note form.

1. How deep did the *Titanic* sink?

   _____

2. Why did the bow sink and the stern rise?

   _____

3. Why did the ship split in two?

   _____

4. What happened to the contents of the ship after it split?

   _____

5. How were the objects from the ship affected by the ocean currents?

   _____

   _____

6. What did Ballard's team look for?

   _____

   _____

7. Where did the team begin its search?

   _____

   _____

8. How did the team carry out its search?

   _____

   _____

Work with a partner to ask and answer the questions. Look back at the reading and indicate where you marked the information.

NOTE-TAKING: CHRONOLOGY OF EVENTS

Scan the reading and find ten to twelve facts about the events Ballard studied in the search for the *Titanic*. Follow the time sequence of these events. Write these facts in note form in the order they occurred.

THE SEARCH FOR THE WRECK OF THE TITANIC

1. April 14, 1912, hit iceberg / opened hole in right side / water rushed in at bow

2. _____
   _____

3. _____
   _____

4. _____
   _____

5. _____
   _____

6. _____
   _____

7. _____
   _____

8. _____
   _____

9. _____
   _____

10. _____
    _____

11. _____
    _____

12. _____
    _____

RECAPPING THE EVENTS

Work with a partner who took notes about the same story. Take turns explaining several of the facts to each other. As you talk, be sure to explain the events in the order they occurred. Check to make sure that you both have the same information. Add or correct any facts you need to.

After Reading

CREATING A TIME LINE

Scan your notes and the reading for dates, times, and the sequence or order of the events in this story of the *Titanic*. Note this information on the following time line.

Event: _____

Time: _____

Event: _____

Time: _____

Work with a partner who prepared a different reading. Make an oral report of these events to your partner. As your partner speaks, note the events your partner reports on and create a time line of the events from both readings.

REACTING TO THE STORY

Return to the discussion questions at the beginning of this chapter. Talk about these questions again. Add new ideas that you learned from the readings. Discuss the additional questions:

1. Do you think the accident could have been avoided? How?
2. Could more people have been saved?
3. What did people learn from this tragedy?

GIVING YOUR OPINION

■ ■

Trying to Raise the Titanic

In August, 1997, an expedition tried to bring up a 10-ton piece of the ship's steel hull to put on public display. They brought the steel hull to within 215 feet (65 meters) of the surface. It looked as though the effort would be successful. Then the unexpected happened. Bad weather moved in, with high winds and stormy seas. The cables holding the steel hull broke under the force of the water. The expedition organizers were discouraged. The weather was not improving, their food was gone, and they had run out of money. They decided to give up and returned to port.

The organizers said that they would return to try again. In 1998 a small section of the ship was raised. There are some, such as Robert Ballard, who say that the ship should be left where it sank both as a piece of history and as a monument to those who died when it sank. Others, such as former U.S. astronaut Edwin Aldrin, say the expedition should continue in order to learn what we can from the mistakes of the past.

Discuss these questions with a partner or with others in a small group.

1. Why are people so interested in the *Titanic* that they would spend millions of dollars to look for it?
2. Should more of the *Titanic* be raised from the sea or left where it is?

Share your opinions with your classmates.

Vocabulary Building

USING CONTEXT CLUES

You can often understand the meaning of a new word from your understanding of the other words in a sentence.

Complete each sentence with one of the following verbs.

a. approached   d. estimated   g. report   i. stared
b. carry   e. explore   h. split   j. traveled
c. created   f. raise

1. The sinking of the *Titanic* _____ panic when it was reported in the news.

2. The builders _____ that it would take about three to five days to sink the *Titanic*.

3. The ship was so big that it took days to _____ it all.

4. The expedition leaders had to _____ enough money to carry out their research.

5. The *Titanic*'s stern rose out of the water and then the ship

   _____ into two pieces.

6. She knew that she had to _____ the accident she had seen.

7. He looked intently and _____ into the darkness trying to find the right road to take.

8. The ship was moving fast, and after a few days it

   _____ the coast of Canada.

9. It was the first time she had ever _____ to another part of the world.

10. There were elevators to _____ people to the different parts of the ship.

DESCRIPTIVE LANGUAGE

Adjectives are words that describe things. Scan the readings in this chapter and notice the different adjectives that are used. Try to find different types of adjectives: those ending in *-er*, like *bigger*; those ending in *-est*, like *biggest*; those ending in *-ing*, like *charming*; and simple adjectives like *gentle*. Find a synonym or antonym for each word on your list. Work with a partner to compare your lists.

Expanding Your Language

SPEAKING

Two-Minute Taped Talk: Choose a part of the *Titanic* story that interests you. It can be about the night the ship sank, the discovery of the ship at the bottom of the ocean, or how you feel about bringing up the *Titanic* from the sea. Based on your own ideas and the information in this chapter, prepare a two-minute audiotape to talk about the *Titanic*. Make a short outline of your ideas in note form. Practice your talk a few times before you record.

WRITING

A. Topic Writing: Use the time line you created to write about what happened to the *Titanic*.

B. Reaction Writing: Write about a part of the *Titanic* story that you find interesting, and tell why it interests you.

The Anasazi:
Why Did They Leave?

Chapter Openers

USING ILLUSTRATIONS TO UNDERSTAND IDEAS

Look at the different activities in the illustrations on the next page. Then read each of the following sentences and write the letter of the activity that matches each sentence.

1. _____ There are beautiful drawings on the walls of the cliff dwellings.

2. _____ The Anasazi built round kivas for religious worship.

3. _____ They made beautiful baskets and pottery.

4. _____ People had to climb up and down steep rocks to reach food and water on the mesa.

5. _____ It was a center of trade and agriculture for the native peoples.

6. _____ The cliff dwellings could be very cold and damp in the winter.

7. _____ The rooms were smoky from the fires needed for warmth and cooking.

8. _____ The Anasazi grew corn, beans, and squash for food.

Work with a partner. Take turns reading each of the statements. Agree on the matches you chose. Then discuss this question:

What do you think were the joys and difficulties of the life shown in these pictures?

Exploring and Understanding Reading

PREDICTING

This reading is about the mystery of why the Anasazi made and abandoned their homes. What do you think you might find out from this reading? List five ideas in note form.

1. How the cliff dwellings were discovered

2. _____

3. _____

4. _____

5. _____

Share your ideas with a partner or with a small group.

SKIMMING

Read all the paragraphs quickly. Add to or change your prediction statements.

SCANNING TO GET THE FACTS

Read the questions after each paragraph. Find the answers in the reading. Underline the key words and write the answers in note form.

■ ■

Mystery of the Southwest

A. Mesa Verde is a flat-topped plateau located in the southwest part of the United States. In this part of the country, the climate is generally dry. The mesa rises up to a height of 8,572 feet (2613 meters). In Spanish, Mesa Verde means "green table." The top of the mesa is covered with green plants and trees. Throughout Mesa Verde there are steep canyons. There is little water at the top of the mesa and even less in the canyons. Water comes from the winter snowfall and spring and summer rains. In the summer temperatures can reach into the 90s (Fahrenheit), but in the winter they can drop to 0 degrees. Today, this area is part of Mesa Verde National Park. The park preserves and protects the culture of the Anasazi people. The beauty and mystery of this place reflect the spirit of those ancient people who once lived here. The park is a World Heritage cultural site and each year is visited by more than 800,000 people from all over the world.

1. Where is Mesa Verde located?

_____

2. Why is Mesa Verde called "green table"?

_____

3. What is the climate of the area like?

_____

4. Where does the water come from?

_____

5. What is the purpose of Mesa Verde National Park?

_____

6. Who visits this area today?

_____

B.   Mesa Verde was the center of life for the Anasazi who lived in the area hundreds of years ago, between the sixth and the fourteenth centuries (A.D. 500–1300). It was a center for trade and agriculture for the native peoples who lived in the Four Corners area of what are today the states of Utah, Colorado, New Mexico, and Arizona. We know very little about the area's history from the 1400s to the late 1800s. In the early 1870s American settlers first began to visit and document their exploration of this area. By the late 1800s ranchers herding their cattle began to wander into the canyons. Here they discovered the ruins of a great lost civilization. They came across magnificent houses made out of the stone under the cliffs of the canyons. Inside they found pottery, baskets, wall art, and tools made from stone. The ranchers were amazed and overwhelmed by the beauty of what they had found. They asked themselves many questions. Who had lived there, and why had these people built homes in the steep canyons? Why did these people leave? Finally, they wondered why the people had abandoned their cliff dwellings.

1. When did the Anasazi live at Mesa Verde?

_____

2. Where was the trade center of native peoples?

_____

3. When did Americans first explore the area?

_____

4. What did the ranchers find in the canyons?

_____

5. a. How did ranchers react to seeing the cliff dwellings?

_____

   b. What questions did they ask themselves?

_____

C.   Soon after the discovery of Mesa Verde, archaeologists came to study the cliff dwellings. They found hundreds of houses built into the sides of the cliffs during the years A.D. 1100 to 1300. The Anasazi had carved out the sandstone rock with simple tools made from stone and wood. Archaeologists have found about six hundred dwellings in the canyons. Some, like Cliff Palace, are very large, but most of the dwellings are smaller in size. There are beautiful drawings on the walls of the cliff dwellings. It appears that the Anasazi would begin their dwellings by constructing round kivas. The kivas are small rooms cut into the ground that people entered from above. They were used for religious worship. The number of these structures show the important role that religion played in Anasazi life. Every building had a kiva. In Cliff Palace there are twenty-three kivas.

1.   How many dwellings have been found in the canyons at Mesa Verde?

   _____

2.   When were the houses built?

   _____

3.   a. How were the kivas constructed?

   _____

   b. What was their purpose?

   _____

4.   How do we know the kivas were important?

   _____

D.   Archaeologists have some ideas about the Anasazi's daily life at Mesa Verde. The early Anasazi were hunter-gatherers. They used wood and stone to make tools—bows and arrows and simple knives for hunting. They ate a simple diet. In the later periods of their civilization, the Anasazi learned to grow corn, beans, and squash. These crops grew well during the long 161–172-day growing season. These foods were a healthy addition to their traditional diet of meat from the deer and bighorn sheep they hunted, and the berries and other plants they gathered. The Anasazi made useful items, like beautiful baskets and pottery covered with distinctive black geometric designs that they used to carry and cook food and water. In the early periods, the Anasazi lived on the top of the mesas.

Then, for some unknown reason, they moved into the canyons. They built new homes under the cliffs. Life in the cliff dwellings was difficult. The rooms were cold and damp in the winter and smoky from the fires needed for warmth and cooking. It was hard to get in and out of their homes. Using only their hands and feet, the Anasazi had to climb up and down the steep rocks to reach food and water on the mesa. This climbing would have been difficult for older people and very dangerous for young children who could fall easily. Most of the Anasazi were under 5 feet tall and generally lived only into their twenties or thirties. The bodies found in the area show that people suffered from medical problems like arthritis, tooth decay, broken bones, and lung disease.

1. What kind of tools did the Anasazi use?

   _____

   _____

2. a. What items did they make for the home?

   _____

   _____

   b. What did they use these items for?

   _____

   _____

3. What was their diet?

   _____

   _____

4. Why did they move from the mesa to the canyons?

   _____

   _____

5. What two things were difficult about living in the cliff dwellings?

   a. _____

   b. _____

6. What medical facts show us that the Anasazi had difficult lives?

   _____

E. By the end of the Great Pueblo period, the Anasazi had moved from smaller cliff dwellings into larger dwellings that could hold a number of families. These larger dwellings were better built and could be defended more easily. Mutual support, increased productivity, and innovation in technology resulted from life in these communal dwellings. The construction of interconnected and large-scale kivas shows an increased emphasis on religion in the Anasazi society. Religious ceremonies might have helped build a spirit of unity among the people. But this great civilization came to an abrupt end sometime between the years 1200 and 1300. The Anasazi abandoned their cliff houses and never returned. What happened to make the Anasazi leave their homes forever is still a mystery today. There are different theories but no certain answers.

1. Why did the Anasazi move into larger dwellings?

   _____

   _____

2. When did the Anasazi leave Mesa Verde?

   _____

   _____

3. What mystery still remains?

   _____

   _____

Work with a partner to ask and answer the questions. Look back at the reading if you cannot agree on the answers.

FINDING THE MAIN IDEAS

Quickly read the beginning and end of each paragraph. Write the main idea of each paragraph in note form, that is, in your own words and in as few words as possible. The main idea of Paragraph A is given as an example.

MAIN IDEAS: MYSTERY OF THE SOUTHWEST

Paragraph A: Description of Mesa Verde

Paragraph B: _____

Paragraph C: _____

Paragraph D: _____

Paragraph E: _____

Work with a partner to compare and refine your ideas. Try to agree on the same ideas. Check your ideas with your teacher.

After Reading

APPLYING THE INFORMATION: THEORIZING

A. Pair or Group Work: Based on the information in the first reading, what could be some reasons that the Anasazi abandoned their homes and never returned? Make a list of theories and choose two or three reasons you can agree on. Share your ideas with your classmates.

B. Individual Work: Read the next paragraphs and highlight the different theories about the Anasazi's departure.

■ ■
―――――――――

The Mystery of the Cliff Dwellers

There are many theories to explain why the Anasazi abandoned their cliff dwellings and left the area. One theory is that they left because a drought occurred and there wasn't enough water to survive. Since the main sources of water were snow and rain, a long period of dry weather could have reduced the water supply. There is evidence that it was extremely dry and cold at this time. Cold weather would have affected the production of corn, the main food source for the Anasazi. Without corn a famine could have begun. Also their farming methods might have caused more food problems. Burning the land and removing all the trees damaged the soil, so less food would grow. Without trees animals may have moved out of the hunting grounds within reach of the Anasazi. Linked to the problem of food supply is the problem of overpopulation. During this period the population had grown, reaching about five thousand. With so many people there probably wasn't a large enough supply of wood to build and make fires.

One controversial theory is that the Anasazi moved into cliff houses to better defend themselves against enemies. There is disagreement over this theory. Those who disagree say there are no physical signs of violence in the area. But those who favor the theory argue that the strong walls and high cliffs brought the Anasazi into the canyons. Any attackers would have had to climb up and down steep rocks to fight. In times of famine (when there is no food) and drought (when there is no water), it is easy to imagine that fighting would start. If this fighting grew too intense or too difficult, then the Anasazi might have decided to abandon the canyons. Added to all this is evidence that the Anasazi could use fires as a system of signaling from different points in the canyons. Perhaps, then, it was possible for groups to communicate with one another. A final theory is that the religious leaders might have convinced the people to move. The increase in the size and amount of kiva construction shows evidence of the greater importance of religion in Anasazi life. Perhaps the priests, who traveled the most between the different groups, convinced the Anasazi that their gods would lead them to a new and better place.

USING HIGHLIGHTING TO MAKE A LIST

From the information that you highlighted, list the theories about why the Anasazi abandoned their cliff dwellings.

1. _____

2. _____

3. _____

4. _____

5. _____

GIVING YOUR OPINION

What theories explaining why the Anasazi left their cliff dwellings do you think are the most believable? Number the theories from most believable (1) to least believable (5). Discuss your list with a partner or with a small group. Try to agree on the order in your group. Report your opinions to your classmates.

DEBATING THE ISSUES TODAY

Recently, park officials in the Southwest have become worried that the large number of tourists will damage the environment and destroy important evidence of ancient life in the areas. For example, bringing cars and other vehicles over dirt roads has caused roads in some places to weaken and wash away in the spring. Using jeeps and other off-road vehicles, people can reach places that were previously undisturbed. Archaeologists are afraid that the tourists will disturb important sites before they can be examined. The danger of fires in these dry areas is also a concern. Some officials think that these areas should be closed or restricted to tourists. Others feel that people should be encouraged to visit national parks for both educational and economic reasons. What is your opinion?

Consider the following idea:

More people should be encouraged to visit National Parks.

Prepare to debate the idea by following the steps in Chapter 16, page 202.

Vocabulary Building

WORD FORMS

Read each sentence and circle the correct word to use in the sentence. Write *N* if the word is a noun or *V* if the word is a verb.

1. _____ The people loved the draw/drawings that the Anasazi carved into the rock.

2. _____ We don't know why people decided to move into the cliff dwell/dwellings.

3. _____ People needed to be strong because climb/climbing the rocks wasn't easy.

4. _____ The survive/survival of the Anasazi depended on having enough food and water for the winter months.

5. _____ Perhaps it was a combine/combination of drought and cold weather that forced the people to move.

6. _____ They needed the cliff dwellings to protect/protection themselves from the cold.

7. _____ The park receives over 800,000 visit/visitors each year.

8. _____ We don't know why the Anasazi decided to abandon/abandonment their cliff dwellings.

9. _____ The Anasazi were able to produce/production beautiful baskets and pottery for use in cooking and carrying water and food.

10. _____ There was a reduce/reduction in the number of animals the Anasazi could find to hunt.

JIGSAW SENTENCES

Use your understanding of key words to match each of the sentence beginnings in Column A with the ending in Column B that fits best.

Column A   Column B

_____ 1. The Anasazi   a. is used for religious
                  civilization   purposes.

_____ 2. Climbing out of   b. is carved out of the
                  the canyons   sandstone rock.

_____ 3. The land   c. is covered with green plants.

_____ 4. The park   d. is divided into different
                                 periods.

_____ 5. Cliff Palace   e. is difficult for old people
                                and children.

_____ 6. The kiva   f. is visited by people from all
                               over the world.

Check your answers in the Answer Key. Take turns reading your answers with a partner.

POSSIBILITY

The words *might, could,* and *would* are verbs or modal forms that show possibility. Many of the theories about the Anasazi are presented as possibilities. Scan the readings and find two sentences with each of these verb or modal forms. Highlight or underline the sentences. Write two sentences of your own using these forms.

Might

1. _____

2. _____

Could

1. _____

2. _____

Would

1. _____

2. _____

Expanding Your Language

SPEAKING

Role-play/Interviewing: Use the notes you made about Mesa Verde and the Life of the Anasazi to role-play an interview between a reporter and an archaeologist. Prepare five or six questions for your partner. Take turns asking these questions and giving answers.

WRITING

Descriptions: Write about a historical place you know of and about what goes on there. Describe the place and the activity there in as much detail as possible.

Read On: Taking It Further

READING SUGGESTIONS

Find some readings or topics like the ones in this unit that you are interested in at your reading level. For example, you could find an easy-reading edition of *The Iceman* by Don Lessem, or of *The Titanic* by Robert Ballard. A good source of reading material is your bookstore or library's magazine and newspaper section.

OTHER SUGGESTIONS

■ *READING TIP: View your reading journal and vocabulary log entries. Review your use of reading skills and strategies. Write a response to the following question: How has your reading improved?*

Television programs have been made about the *Titanic*, the Iceman, and the Anasazi. Movies have been made about the *Titanic*. Try to find out if one of these programs or movies is available through your library or video store. Ask your teacher for help in locating these programs and watching them. Talk about what you watched with your classmates.

Answer Key

CHAPTER 1   Where Does the Time Go?

Previewing, page 6

(sample answers) **1.** Different suggestions on how to study better, etc.   **2.** Time management techniques that will help you to study better.   **3.** College or university students.

Understanding Details, page 8

1. b "As you read, underline, circle, or otherwise note the suggestions you think you can use."
2. c "Many people learn best in daylight hours"   **3.** c ". . . you train your body to be alert at your desk. . ."   **4.** a "Most people can get more done in a shorter time at the library."   **5.** b "The overwhelming majority of research indicated that silence is the best form of music for study."

Note-Taking; Listing Key Words and Phrases, page 9

A. Get off the phone
  1. ultimate interrupter
  2. call at worst time
  3. unplug the phone
  4. get an answering machine
  5. study at the library.

B. Avoid noise distraction
  1. avoid television
  2. turn off stereo
  3. silence best
  4. ask if study rooms available
  5. go somewhere quiet.

Vocabulary in Context, page 11

1. d   **2.** i   **3.** b   **4.** c   **5.** a   **6.** h   **7.** e   **8.** j   **9.** g   **10.** f

Sentence Form, page 12

(sample answers) **1.** *Use* a regular study area   **2.** *Study* when you'll be alert   **3.** *Get* off the phone
4. *Learn* to say no   **5.** *Avoid* noise distraction.

CHAPTER 2   The Habits of a Lifetime—Are We Affected?

Predicting, page 15

(sample answers) **3.** What their family history was   **4.** How old they are now

Understanding Details, pages 16–18

Paragraph A
1. In a one-room wood house near the village of Brownsbranch, forty miles away from Springfield, Missouri.
2. With a wood stove.
3. She collects rain water.
4. In 1916.
5. **a.** She doesn't have electricity, running water, or indoor plumbing.   **b.** She heats her house and cooks her food on a wood stove.   **c.** She uses an outhouse.   **d.** She cooks her own food from a few supplies that she buys in the village.   **e.** She keeps food cold in a special underground cellar next to her house.

Paragraph B
1. She was six years old.
2. Because they heard that there was good land and lots of water available for farming.
3. **a.** 120 acres   **b.** $800
4. He raised crops, chickens, and cattle.
5. One of Birdle's sisters died in the flu epidemic of 1918, her brother died in 1926, and her father died in 1936. They acquired only a few modern conveniences; they had a pick-up truck, a portable radio, and in 1970 got a telephone installed. Her mother died in 1969, and her sister in 1972.
6. After her mother and sister died, Birdle was left alone and had to manage on her own.

Paragraph C
1. She had gone to college and trained to be a teacher. She taught school in two of the villages near her home. She also taught Sunday school and wrote local news reports for two area newspapers.
2. A person can't do everything in life, so do what makes you happy.
3. They worry that at 87 Birdle is too old to be living by herself.
4. She's not yet ready to leave her house in the woods. She says, "I can still cut my own wood and pump my own water. In my mind and heart, I don't feel old."

Understanding Details, pages 21–23

Paragraph A
1. One of the world's oldest people.
2. In 1997.
3. **a.** About her memories.   **b.** To tell them the secret of her long life.
4. They hoped that they could find the key to living a long and active life.

Paragraph B
1. In Arles, a city in southern France.
2. Unfortunately, her husband, daughter, and only grandson all died before her, leaving her to live alone.
3. She ate chocolate almost every day.   **b.** She liked to smoke.   **c.** She also liked to drink a glass of wine with her noon meal.   **d.** She rubbed her skin with olive oil.
4. **a.** She rode a bicycle.   **b.** She took a brisk, long walk every day.

Paragraph C
1. Her mother lived to be 86; her father lived to be 93.
2. She had a positive attitude toward life.
3. **a.** In her later years she couldn't see or hear people because she had become deaf and blind.
   b. She still felt she had something to be happy about every day.

Synonyms, page 25

1. warm   **2.** safety   **3.** make   **4.** questioning   **5.** outlook   **6.** busy   **7.** unhearing
8. fast

Antonyms, page 26

1. i   **2.** d   **3.** b   **4.** f   **5.** g   **6.** a   **7.** h   **8.** c   **9.** e

CHAPTER 3   The Power of Naps

Information from a Graph, page 29

1. At 4 P.M.   **2.** 2 P.M.: 60, 9 A.M.: 20, 6 P.M.: 30

Getting the Main Idea, page 32

Paragraph A: Some information about our body's natural sleep rhythms.
Paragraph B: The decrease in the amount of time people are sleeping.
Paragraph C: The problem of tired workers and some solutions to this problem.
Paragraph D: Some advice for people who want to take a nap in the afternoon.

Scanning: Getting the Facts, page 32

A. 1. T   **2.** T   **3.** T   **4.** F   **5.** T
B. 1. aren't   **2.** don't   **3.** more   **4.** two   **5.** do   **6.** faster

Applying Information: Using Facts to Make a Case, page 34

(sample answers) **1.** for napping on the job, six school caretakers have been told to leave their work; suspensions ranged from a week to a month without pay; inspectors found one worker sleeping under a blanket and with a pillow, another worker had an alarm clock, etc.
2. Let workers have regular breaks where they could nap for 20 minutes, for example.

Word Forms, page 35

1. a. sleep,   **b.** sleepy   **2. a.** moody,   **b.** mood   **3. a.** day,   **b.** daily   **4. a.** difficult,
b. difficulty   **5. a.** nightly,   **b.** night

Synonyms, page 36

1. c   **2.** f   **3.** d   **4.** e   **5.** j   **6.** a   **7.** i   **8.** g   **9.** b   **10.** h

CHAPTER 4   What's in a Name?

Previewing, page 45

(sample predictions) **1.** Why first names are important to us.   **2.** How our names affect our lives.
3. Examples of different traditions for family names.

Getting the Main Idea, page 46

Paragraph A: Some traditions in choosing first names.
Paragraph B: The effects that names can have on people's lives.
Paragraph C: The traditions of family names in different countries.

Scanning: Getting the Facts, page 47

1. a. name child after a relative   **b.** pleasant-sounding name   **c.** name child after a famous or popular person
2. a. They can be favored over others with less popular names.   **b.** They can be teased or made fun of.
3. a. To make life easier for them.   **b.** To be more successful in their jobs.
4. China: People use their family name first and their given name second.   Spanish-speaking countries: Children take the family name of both parents.   Denmark: Two-thirds of the population use only 50 family names.

Note-taking, page 48

(sample answers)

FIRST NAMES
• after a relative
• after a famous person
• pleasant sounding
• popular name

FAMILY NAMES
• last name first (China)
• both parents' names (Spanish-speaking countries)
• many people with same name (Denmark)
• immigrants may change their name

Vocabulary in Context, page 50

1. d **2.** a **3.** c **4.** g **5.** b **6.** f **7.** e

Synonyms, page 50

1. let **2.** select **3.** alter **4.** make **5.** choose **6.** get **7.** reject **8.** record

CHAPTER 5 Researching our Hidden Roots

Information Questions, page 55

1. Three people. John was an only child.
2. He found legal papers and newspaper clippings.
3. a. He was adopted. **b.** He had a twin sister.
4. a. He was going to find his sister. **b.** He was going to go to the hospital where he was born.

Note-taking, page 56

• lived in Albany, NY
• not much contact with family
• parents died in car accident
• decided to sell the house
• found legal papers

• discovered he was adopted
• had a twin sister
• felt angry
• began to search for his sister

Information questions, page 58

1. She got married.
2. She was overjoyed about her pregnancy but worried.
3. a. He asked about her family medical history. **b.** She didn't know many of the answers and was uncomfortable and embarrassed.
4. a. The information will help her have a healthy pregnancy. **b.** He could identify medical problems the unborn baby might have.
5. a. Genetically transmitted diseases. **b.** Miscarriages or premature births. **c.** Multiple births.
6. Joy was going to ask her parents and in-laws questions.

Note-taking, page 59

• just moved from Chicago to San Francisco
• found out she was pregnant
• overjoyed, a little worried
• far from her family/asked for recommendations

• chose doctor near home
• made appointment
• because new patient, doctor asked questions about medical history of her relatives
• didn't have a lot of answers, etc.

Comparing the Stories, page 60

(sample answers) **1.** John wants to find his sister, who was born at the same time as he was. Joy wants to find out more about her family's medical background because she is pregnant. **2.** They both have questions to answer, important information to look for. They have different reasons for finding out about their past, etc.

Vocabulary in Context, page 60

1. d   **2.** a   **3.** c   **4.** b   **5.** e   **6.** g   **7.** f

Word Forms, page 61

1. a. pregnancy,   **b.** pregnant   **2. a.** genetic,   **b.** genetically   **3. a.** question,
b. questioned   **4. a.** memorabilia,   **b.** remember,   **c.** memories

CHAPTER 6   Writing Our Own History

Personalizing, page 63

(sample answers) **2.** her birth certificate   **3.** pictures of her parents, brothers and sisters, or herself
4. letters from friends, parents, boyfriend, husband

Previewing, page 65

(sample answers) **1.** The personal life stories of different people   **2.** How to write our own stories
3. Why writing our autobiographies helps us record our memories and stay connected

Skimming, page 65

1. To write about yourself, your autobiography.
2. It is a precious legacy, we all have a story to tell, and we owe it to others to share our experiences. It helps us to remember our relatives and gives us an appreciation of what it's like to live a long and happy life. It reminds us of our grandparents.

Checking the facts, pages 67–68

A.
1. F   "From her grandmother who is no longer living"
2. T   "She began to lead workshops on the art of memoir writing."
3. F   "They feel their life has been terribly ordinary and is not likely to be of interest to anyone else."
4. T   "The hardest part of autobiographical writing is getting started."
5. T   "I can flip through her scrapbook and reflect on her memories of yesteryear."

B.
1. a. Her feelings about the grandfather she never knew.   **b.** The joys and wonder of caring for her babies when they were young.   **c.** Witnessed world events like the end of World War I.
2. She is a freelance writer.
3. a. childhood   **b.** school days   **c.** career   **d.** marriage   **e.** childbearing   **f.** retirement
4. b. a scrapbook.   **c.** piecing your materials together.   **d.** photos, artwork, report cards, ticket stubs, wedding invitations, and other memorabilia that are significant to you.   **e.** the memories that they trigger for you.
5. a. We all have a story to tell (or it helps us to remember).   **b.** We owe it to others to share our experiences (or to get an appreciation of what it's like to live a long and happy life).

Relating Main Ideas and Details, page 69

A. Paragraph starting with "One of Mary Bolton's greatest treasure is a scrapbook . . ."
B. Paragraph starting with "Bolton, 33, a freelance writer . . ."
C. Paragraph starting with "Bolton says that the hardest part of creating a scrapbook is getting started . . ."
D. Paragraph starting with "While creating a scrapbook can be time-consuming . . ."

Applying the information: Discovering the Reasons People Write, page 69

A, C, D

Vocabulary in Context, page 71

1. genealogy/family history; **2.** memorabilia/different items from the past; **3.** witness/like the end of World War I; **4.** reluctant/hesitate; **5.** chronologically/fit into major periods of your life; **6.** legacy/helps me to remember.

Word Forms: Roots, page 72

1. memories **2.** memorabilia **3.** remember **4.** memoir.

Matching Meanings, page 72

1. d **2.** e **3.** a **4.** c **5.** b **6.** f

CHAPTER 7 Starting Young—Learning the Value of Money

Skimming, page 78

C. Parents should give their children different advice about money depending on their age.

Understanding Details, page 80

1. a **2.** b **3.** a **4.** b **5.** c **6.** a

Applying the Information: Problem Solving, page 81

1. Help him or her compare the cost of different schools; talk about ways to pay for the high tuition (applying for a loan, getting a summer job).
2. Tell her/him that s/he can buy it if s/he saves enough money.
3. Suggest that s/he open a checking account, tell her that she can pay for part of her school expenses with the money she earns.
4. Suggest that s/he put the money in a savings account.

Evaluating the Information, page 82

(sample answers) **1.** (Your opinion) **a.** He greets customers as president of the Children's Bank at Enterprise Bank of Omaha. **b.** How to apply for loans, how business deposits work. **c.** (Your opinion)

Vocabulary in Context, page 83

1. a **2.** e **3.** b **4.** d **5.** c

Giving More Advice: Sentence Form, page 84

1. *Give* a small allowance each week. **2.** *Increase* their allowance gradually. **3.** *Talk* about ways to earn extra money. **4.** *Have* children open a checking account. **5.** *Save* money for future schooling.

CHAPTER 8   Lotteries—Good for Society?

Getting Information from a Graph, page 88

1. Large jackpots   **2.** (Your opinion)

Skimming, page 89

Positive: because the people won the lottery when they were in serious financial trouble and most lottery winners were happy with the results.

Scanning, pages 89–92

Paragraph A:
1. a. People earn a little under $20,000 a year.   **b.** The population is small.
2. Most jobs pay minimum wage.
3. a. Drought.   **b.** Falling cattle prices.
4. They thought that it would be the last Thanksgiving in their homes.

Paragraph B:
1. A group of 43 townspeople each won part of a $46.7 million dollar prize in the Texas state lottery.
2. They joined the lottery pool by putting in $10 each. They bought 430 tickets.
3. They won $40,000 a year for the next 20 years.
4. a. They plan to pay off the debts on their farms.   **b.** One man said the money would enable him to keep on farming instead of looking for a second job.
5. a. They're not planning on taking expensive vacations.   **b.** They're not planning on buying luxury homes.

Paragraph C:
1. There are lotteries in at least 37 states and in the District of Columbia.
2. More than $88 million.
3. a. $20 billion   **b.** $10 billion

Recapping the story, page 92

(sample notes) population only about 600, most people farmers, most jobs minimum wage, bad luck, drought, falling prices for cattle, serious financial trouble, worried banks going to take away their farms, Thanksgiving weekend 1997, thought it would be the last in their homes, etc.

Scanning, pages 93–96

Paragraph A
1. A successful businessman who owned a small restaurant.
2. He loves to gamble.
3. Up to $250 a day.
4. a. He lost his restaurant and his job.   **b.** He found himself more than $1 million in debt.
    c. His wife divorced him.
5. He tried to commit suicide.

Paragraph B
1. For three weeks.
2. join a self-help group, Gamblers Anonymous.
3. a. He got the support of professionals who helped him find a job.   **b.** He also got financial help.
4. a. Andy stopped buying lottery tickets.   **b.** He is able to help pay for his children's university tuition bills.   **c.** His children believe in him and respect him.

5. Happy—he is realizing he can get the peace and happiness he always wanted without having to win a lottery.

Paragraph C

1. **a.** Spend money.　**b.** Steal money.
2. TYPE　　　　　　　　EXAMPLE
   　a. Financial problems　**a.** Bankruptcy, job loss
   　b. Health problems　　**b.** Depression, suicide
   　c. Social problems　　**c.** Divorce, jail time
3. **a.** It can only be estimated.　**b.** Into the billions of dollars.
4. Are lotteries a good way for governments to raise money?

Recapping the Story, page 97

(sample notes) married with two children, loved to gamble, would spend vacations and weekends at casinos, made over $100,000 a year, in 1982 bought first lottery ticket, spending up to $250 a day, over eight years he lost over $100,000 on lottery tickets, etc.

Matching Meanings, page 98

1. f　**2.** g　**3.** j　**4.** d　**5.** b　**6.** i　**7.** h　**8.** a　**9.** e　**10.** c

Synonyms, page 99

1. permit　**2.** exit　**3.** commit　**4.** understand　**5.** use up

CHAPTER 9　The Future of Money

Predicting, page 101

1. T　**2.** T　**3.** T　**4.** T　**5.** T

Skimming, page 101

B. There are advantages and disadvantages in using bank cards instead of cash.

Recognizing Sub-points, page 103

1. D　**2.** S　**3.** S　**4.** D　**5.** D　**6.** D

Discussion Questions, page 105

(sample answers) **1.** She asks people with spare change to send in their pennies to raise money for her charity.　**2.** Yes, she's looking to raise even more money.　**3.** Because when it comes to pennies, most folks consider them a nuisance and just want to get rid of them.　**4.** (Your opinion)

Expressions, page 105

A. 1. d　**2.** a　**3.** e　**4.** b　**5.** c
B. (Varies)

Vocabulary in Context, page 106

1. j　**2.** c　**3.** f　**4.** e　**5.** h　**6.** g　**7.** b　**8.** d　**9.** a　**10.** i

CHAPTER 10   Something's Happening at the Zoo

Personalizing, page 112

(sample answers): **1.** What kinds of animals do you keep in your zoo?   **2.** Do you keep animals in cages? Why or why not?   **3.** How is your zoo different from traditional zoos?   **4.** What are the advantages of zoos?

Skimming, page 113

a. favors the work done in modern zoos.

Understanding Explanations, page 115

1. Inside a bear's cage, zoos can recreate the forest with some of the different kinds of plants, tree trunks, and waterfalls. They can also give the animals places where they can be private and hide away from people.
2. a. They try to make the animals work for their food. They put seeds and other food in different parts of their enclosure so that they have to look for the food.   **b.** They freeze fish pieces in ice cubes so the animal has to break the ice to get the food.
3. a. People try to give food or throw things into the animal's cages that can harm them, like plastic wrappers or candy.   **b.** Animals can get sick if they come into contact with people. Viruses from people can affect animals too.
4. They help wild animals reproduce in the safety of a zoo.
5. They have to see that the animal can survive.

Note-taking: Listing Advantages, page 116

1. The enclosures feel like home with different plants, tree trunks, waterfalls.
2. Animals spend more time looking for food.
3. Animals can hide when they want to.
4. Zoos can conserve animals that are endangered and return them to the wild.

Applying the Information: Making a Decision, page 117

(sample reasons) *For:* **1.** Keiko is not well enough to be released.   **2.** Keiko could never survive in the wild.   *Against:* **1.** Keiko is healthy enough to be released.   **2.** Wild animals should not live in zoos or aquariums.

Vocabulary in Context: Jigsaw sentences, page 119

1. b   **2.** c   **3.** a

Adjectives, page 119

1. e   **2.** d   **3.** c   **4.** a   **5.** b

CHAPTER 11   The Return of the Wolves

Skimming, page 122

No: "Some people argued in favor and some against the reintroduction of wolves."

Paragraph A
1. In the West of the United States; the Rocky Mountains run through the park. The park is 2.3 million acres.
2. Elk, buffalo, and bear. You can't find the gray wolf.

3. From northern Mexico to Greenland.
4. They were hunted down and completely eliminated.
5. a. The U.S. government passed a law that made it possible to return wolves to Yellowstone.
  b. The U.S. Fish and Wildlife Service first suggested a plan to move ten breeding pairs of wolves to the park.

Paragraph B
1. Seventeen wolves captured in Canada were released into Yelowstone Park.
2. a. They were concerned that the animals might die as a result of the move.   **b.** They were concerned that the wolves would be killed by hunters or ranchers in the United States.
3. a. They will hunt their livestock.   **b.** They could attack small children and domestic animals.
  c. The federal government should not be spending taxpayers' dollars to return wolves to Yellowstone.

Paragraph C
1. a. They play an important part in the ecosystem.   **b.** Through their hunting they remove the weak and diseased members of the elk and deer populations.   **c.** They keep the elk and deer populations from growing too large.
2. The naturalists want tourists to hear wolves howl at night.

Recapping the Information: Highlighting, page 125

(sample highlighting answers) **1.** 1600s: wolves, northern Mexico to Greenland / killed, when people moved in, settled, United States (etc.)
2. 1995, seventeen wolves released, Yellowstone / ranchers, farmers, against returning wolves (etc.)

Reacting to the Information, page 126

(sample answers) **1.** Wolves play an important role in the ecosystem; wolves keep the deer and the elk populations from growing too large, etc.   **2.** (Your opinion)

Skimming, page 127

No: Ranchers, farmers, and hunters object to the reintroduction . . .

Paragraph A
1. a. Powerful jaws   **b.** They have been known to track, or follow, animals for many miles.
2. a. Out of 131 times scientists recorded wolves following moose, the wolves attacked the moose only 7 times.   **b.** Wolves killed only 6 times out of 131 animals that they tracked.   **c.** Animals can and do defend themselves against wolves.
3. A dominant female and a dominant male, several males and females, and pups; led by a dominant female.

Paragraph B
1. a. There are no records of any healthy wolves attacking people in North America.   **b.** There are a few reports of wolves scratching or biting people, but no reports of serious injuries.
2. a. They will attack dogs and other domestic pets.   **b.** They will attack livestock such as cattle or sheep. On average they kill three cattle per thousand each year.
3. They will capture and remove them.
4. They are removed and killed.
5. The government pays ranchers if any of their cows or sheep are killed by wolves. The highest amount paid in one year to ranchers was $21,000.

Paragraph C

1. The effect of returning wolves on the ecology of Yellowstone to see if the area would benefit from the reintroduction or if it would damage the balance of nature.
2. Ranchers, farmers, and hunters.
3. For the Canadian wolves to be removed from Yellowstone.
4. From 33 to 97.
5. They have killed coyotes and elk. As a result, other animals, such as bears, rodents, hawks, and bald eagles, have survived in the park.
6. More time is needed to see if there are proven benefits and if the wolves will be allowed to stay.

Recapping the Information: Highlighting, page 130

(sample highlighted answers) **1.** Strong, powerful jaws, track animals for miles / not needlessly attack, kill, etc.   **2.** experiment, effect on ecology, benefit or damage balance of nature / ranchers, farmers, hunters object, etc.

Reacting to the Information, page 130

(sample answers) **1.** Yes and no. No: Wolves are not dangerous to humans. Wolves do not needlessly kill other animals. Yes: Wolves will attack dogs, domestic animals, livestock, etc.   **2.** Yes, studies show that the return of wolves has benefited the environment of the park. A greater variety of other animals, like bears, rodents and hawks, have survived, etc.   **3.** (Your opinion).

Applying the Information: Using Facts to Make an Argument, page 131

(sample arguments) *For:* They play an important part in the ecosystem. Through their hunting they remove the weak and diseased members of the elk and deer populations. Wolves are not dangerous to people. They do not needlessly kill other animals, etc.
Against: Hunters are afraid that wolves will prey on the elk and kill so much that there won't be enough left for them to hunt. They will attack livestock such as cattle or sheep: on average they kill three per thousand each year, etc.

Vocabulary Building: Word Forms, page 132

1. **a.** consult,   **b.** consultation
2. **a.** discussion,   **b.** discuss
3. **a.** elimination,   **b.** eliminate
4. **a.** oppose,   **b.** opposition
5. **a.** introduction,   **b.** introduce

CHAPTER 12   Protecting Water Resources

Previewing Graphic Information, page 136

1. a.   **2.** a

Skimming, page 140

1. Desalination of sea and ocean water.   **2.** Using solar energy instead of fossil fuels for desalination plants.   **3.** Transporting water to needy regions.

Scanning for Specific Information, pages 140–142

A. 1. Only about 2.5 percent.
  2. 99 percent is located in glaciers and permanent snow covers or in unrenewable underground aquifers.

3. Less than 1 percent.
4. Freshwater lakes and rivers.
5. In the Persian Gulf countries.
6. **a.** The Balearic Islands of Spain. **b.** Malta.
7. A lot would disappear on the way through warmer waters. You would have to be able to stock it somewhere.
8. **a.** Non-drinking water uses. **b.** Irrigation of parks, golf courses, and freeway landscaping.
   c. Use in cooling towers, boilers, and certain water-intensive industries.
9. About 100 million gallons a day.

B. 1. unfit "the problem is that almost 98 percent of it is salt water—unfit to drink . . ."
   2. nonrenewable "Some groundwater sources can be tapped, but most of the water they contain is nonrenewable . . ."
   3. unfeasible "More important, the high cost of desalination makes it unfeasible for many developing countries . . ."
   4. unfeasible "But solar power is not feasible in many water-scarce countries."
   5. unaffordable "Many proposals focus on transporting water." ". . . but so far we do not have one that is sufficiently affordable."
   6. non-drinking "California's Central Basin district, for example, uses wastewater that has gone through several treatment cycles for a number of non-drinking water uses."
   7. encourage ". . . but experts agree that something must be done to encourage greater water conservation around the world."

Note-taking: Advantages and Disadvantages, page 142

Solution 1. Desalination. *Advantage:* Limitless quantity. *Disadvantage:* not all water-scarce countries have access to water, the high cost makes it unfeasible for many developing countries.
Solution 2. Solar power to power desalination plants. *Advantage:* An alternative to fossil fuels (for example, in Massawa, Ethiopia, it provides enough fresh water for 500 people). *Disadvantage:* not feasible in many water-scarce countries.
Solution 3. Transporting water. *Advantage:* Feasible in countries with relatively strong economies. *Disadvantage:* Not feasible in weaker economies, not sufficiently affordable.

Applying the Information: Identifying a Plan, page 143

A. A plan to recycle wastewater.

Understanding Details in an Extended Example, page 145

1. A small, affordable system to clean wastewater on a very local scale; the "Living Machines"
2. Wastewater that comes from toilets, baths, dishwashers, washing machines, and any other home plumbing system.
3. **a.** In a big plastic tank where bacteria start to remove the waste. **b.** In a greenhouse filled with plants, fish, and algae that feed on it.
4. With the help of sunlight and the plants and animals.
5. **a.** Washing, flushing toilets, bathing, watering the lawn, washing the dog, swimming.
   b. Drinking or cooking.
6. It costs the same as a commercial septic system. The local government saves tax money it would spend to transport waste to large recycling plants.
7. Wastewater is not put into the fresh water supply system. It could help reduce the amount of fresh water we need to take from lakes and rivers.

Vocabulary in Context, page 146

1. unfit to drink; bring in bottled water   **2.** locked up/couldn't use   **3.** non-renewable, finite resource   **4.** desalination; access to seawater   **5.** needy; regions rely   **6.** generates revenue; pay for water and food   **7.** stock up; in a safe place   **8.** irrigation of parks; use recycled water

Synonyms, page 147

1. j   **2.** g   **3.** b   **4.** i   5 .c   **6.** a   **7.** h   **8.** e   **9.** d   **10.** f

Word Forms, page 147

1. a. conserve,   **b.** conservation   **2. a.** solve,   **b.** solution   **3. a.** pollution,   **b.** pollute
4. a. desalinate,   **b.** desalination   **5. a.** reduce,   **b.** reduction   **6.** a. irrigate,   **b.** irrigation

Words with the Prefix **re-***, page 149*

1. limitless, always replenished, it never runs out   **2.** to fill up again   **3.** to take away, separate
4. to use again

CHAPTER 13   The Importance of Friendship

Predicting, page 155

(sample predictions) **1.** Who is involved in the story.   **2.** Where and when the story took place.
3. Short explanations about what happened in the story.   **4.** Reasons why the story is important.

Previewing, page 155

(sample answers) **1.** A story about how a group of friends helped one of their friends.   **2.** What was Soo Yeun Kim's problem.   **3.** How the students at Jericho High school helped Soo Yeun Kim.
4. The location of Jericho High School.

Skimming, page 157

After she was killed in an accident, her classmates filled out the application to enter the science project she had completed for the Westinghouse Science Talent Search.

Chronology: Following the Story, page 157

a. 3   **b.** 8   **c.** 2   **d.** 1   **e.** 6   **f.** 7   **g.** 5   **h.** 4

Understanding Descriptive Details. page 158

1. She was "an accomplished flutist, editor of the literary magazine, and a star science student."
2. He was one of Jericho's "best and brightest students."
3. It was "a two-year study of bone fragments as they related to the behavior of the Neanderthal man."
4. "What awards had she won? What clubs did she belong to?" and "What would you really like to be doing 10 or 15 years from now?"
5. It was "torn off."
6. They are described as "selfless."

Applying the Information: Similarities and Differences, page 159

1. Yes, she did.
2. No, he was totally surprised by the offer and didn't know how to respond.
3. They started spending more and more time together during the six weeks it took to see if they were a match, sparks began to fly, and by the time the results came in the romance was under way.

4. The negative part is that Ken had been sick for so long and that both would have to be operated on. The positive part is that Carol Fleck donated her kidney to a friend and that she fell in love with him and married him before the transplant took place.

Vocabulary in Context, page 161

1. b   **2.** a   **3.** c   **4.** a   **5.** c   **6.** c

Word Forms, page 162

1. application, applicable   **2.** finish, final   **3.** accomplishments, accomplished   **4.** (noun) award   **5.** competition, competitive   **6.** operation, operable   **7.** involvement, involved

CHAPTER 14   Living With Our Emotions

Previewing for the General Topic, page 165

D. Shyness: effects, reasons, and some ways to overcome it.

Main Ideas of Paragraphs, page 166

1. C   **2.** A   **3.** B

Note-taking: Recognizing Supporting Points and Details, page 167

B. Different causes of shyness
1. *Genetic cause of shyness:* 15 percent are shy from birth. The hearts of shy children beat much faster. They are nervous, afraid of new experiences, blush, become embarrassed, shake with fear when faced with new people and experiences.
2. *Genes influenced by experience:* Positive: help child develop self-esteem or self-worth. Parent or caring adult can offer experiences that show child how important he or she is. Chance to develop an ability, gain skill and confidence to overcome shyness. Early experiences change structures in brain. Parent's praise of child's accomplishments; tolerance for failure.
C. Shyness in adults
1. *Ways to introduce themselves and join in conversation:* Find common ground for conversation by relating shared experiences. Asking questions. Learn how to ask others about themselves. Prepare by having topics of universal interest.
2. *Techniques for speaking to others:* Write down question to ask. Plan what to say. Write dialogue. Practice beginning lines.
3. *Listening to other:* Active listening techniques. Learn to listen in informal conversation. Make a mental note of a person's interest. Listen to the way people begin or end conversations and choose lines to use in similar situations.
4. *Relaxation techniques:* Slow breathing. Thinking about a positive memory.

Answering questions from notes, page 168

1. F   About 15 percent
2. F   "Most children who are born shy lose their shyness over time"
3. T   "A shy child who is given the chance to develop an ability . . . will gain the skills and the confidence to overcome shyness"
4. T   "They can learn specific ways to introduce themselves and join in conversations"
5. F   "Active listening techniques are useful in overcoming shyness"
6. T   "Relaxation techniques . . . are useful ways to reduce fear of contact with others"

Previewing for the General Topic, page 169

D. Worrying: effect, reasons, and ways to cope with it

Main Ideas of Paragraphs, page 170

1. C   **2.** A   **3.** B

Note-taking: Recognizing Supporting Points and Details, page 171

A. How worry affects us
1. *Everyday worries:* Deadlines. Financial problems. Relationships with others.
2. *Benefits of worrying:* Not always a bad thing. Time to concentrate on a problem, find possible solutions or ways to deal with it. Stimulating, propels us to do better work or complete work on time.
3. *Problems with worrying:* Uncomfortable. Interferes with problem-solving ability. Stops us from taking steps needed to solve the problem. Saps energy. Leads to physical problems: fatigue, headaches, muscle pain, insomnia.

B. Techniques to cope with everyday worrying
1. *Technique 1:* "Progressive Relaxation": Lie down, tighten and relax parts of the body until totally relaxed, once or twice a day, 10 minutes.
2. *Technique 2:* Regular meditation: Sit, close eyes, repeat simple, pleasing sound, twice a day, 20 minutes.
3. *Problem-solving techniques:* Unproductive mental energy thinking, "I'll never solve this problem," "this is too much for me." Professional counselors, therapists help. Change negative message, replace with positive thoughts.

Answering Questions from Notes, page 172

1. T   **2.** T   **3.** F   **4.** T   **5.** T

Adjectives to Nouns, page 175

1. a. shy,   **b.** shyness   **2. a.** encourage,   **b.** encouragement   **3. a.** relaxed,   **b.** relaxation
4. a. perfect,   **b.** perfection   **5. a.** nervous,   **b.** nervousness

Synonyms, page 176

1. n   **2.** h   **3.** j   **4.** l   **5.** o   **6.** c   **7.** a   **8.** i   **9.** e   **10.** b   **11.** m   **12.** k
13. d   **14.** f   **15.** g

Antonyms, page 177

1. uncomfortable/comfortable
2. uneasy/at ease or comfortable
3. unfortunately/fortunately
4. unproductive/productive
5. unlikely/likely

CHAPTER 15 Handwriting and Our Personality

Info-Gap: Getting Information from Diagrams, page 180

Set A: **1.** A   Lines are uneven;   **2.** B   Circle is in the middle of the page;   **3.** B   There is a space separating "am" from 36. This shows hesitation;   **4.** A   The name Jack is written larger. This shows a positive feeling towards the person.

Set B: **5.** B   Small script is a sign of intelligence;   **6.** A   The numbers in "A" are not written clearly;   **7.** B   The line through the last name indicates displeasure;   **8.** A   Not following the margins shows disrespect for rules.

Skimming, page 182

(sample answers)   **1.** Graphology is the study of all forms of graphic movement.
2. Graphologists use five tools in analyzing written or graphic work.   **3.** Businesses are using handwriting analysis as a tool to choose their new employees.

Scanning for Details, page 185

A. 1. all forms of graphic movement including drawing and doodling   **2.** legitimate science, seriously   **3.** conscious, unconscious   **4.** five different tools

B.
1. country/region of origin, level of intelligence, emotional stability, aptitudes and talents, leadership qualities, honesty level, physical activity level, work/school performance, alcoholism/drug abuse
2. Certain movements of the pen, the way the size or style of handwriting changed, or if an unusual amount of space was left between words in a sentence.
3. **a.** Physical signs, psychological signs, universal concepts, common sense signs, scientific method.
   b. Physical signs: When writer's hand shakes, the writing shakes. A tense and nervous writer will push harder on the page. Illness, dishonesty, drug or alcohol abuse. Person is trying to hide his or her true identity.
   c. Psychological signs: Graphologists must understand basic psychological theory to make an interpretation. If a person overdoes something it means opposite is true. (If the word *Love,* for example, is written larger than the rest it means the writer does not feel love).
   d. Universal concepts: Universal body movements showing emotions; assume a link between move-ment and emotion. A person who writes with upward motion feels happy. A person who writes big feels important.
   e. Common sense signs: a person who is neat and tidy writes in an orderly way. People who don't like their names will not write their signature clearly.
   f. Scientific method: Study large numbers of handwriting samples. Get writing samples from spe-cial groups of people, compare samples to samples from general population. Criminals do not begin their sentences at the left-hand margin, identified 25 handwriting traits more common among criminals.
4. **a.** As a way to find the right employee, to help decide promotions and other job changes.
   b. It saves thousands of dollars in lost time and training.

Applying the Information, page 187

b. indirectly

Word Forms, page 190

A. psychiatrist: a person who practices psychiatry, who does therapy
   graphologist: a person who studies all forms of graphic movement
   anthropologist: a person who studies cultures
B. 1. intelligent   **2.** spacious/spatial   **3.** emotional   **4.** psychological   **5.** psychiatric
   6. criminal   **7.** important

Antonyms, page 191

(sample antonyms) **1.** unusual, usual   **2.** dishonesty, honesty   **3.** inconsistent, consistent
4. unexpectedly, expectedly

CHAPTER 16   The Mystery of the Iceman

Predicting, page 196

(sample predictions) **2.** who discovered him   **3.** why he died   **4.** a description of the man
5. why this discovery is important

Skimming, page 196

It will give us a much more complete picture of the daily life of ancient people who lived 5,300 years ago.

Chronology: Following the Story, page 199

a. 5   **b.** 3   **c.** 9   **d.** 8   **e.** 11   **f.** 1   **g.** 7   **h.** 2   **i.** 6   **j.** 4   **k.** 10

Understanding Descriptive Details, page 200

B. 1. d   **2.** f   **3.** h   **4.** e   **5.** c   **6.** b   **7.** a   **8.** g
C. What was the purpose of the tattoos? Were they religious symbols or the mark of a brave leader or hunter? What diseases had he had? How did he die? How have human genes changed over the centuries?

Vocabulary in Context, page 202

1. e   **2.** i   **3.** b   **4.** j   **5.** a   **6.** g   **7.** f   **8.** h   **9.** d   **10.** c

Jigsaw Sentences, page 203

1. b   **2.** d   **3.** c   **4.** a

Word Forms, page 204

Hiker: a person who likes to hike or go for long walks in nature
Scientist: a person who works in science
Photographer: a person who works taking pictures
Reporter: a journalist, a person who writes for a newspaper, a newsmagazine, or a television news show
Archaeologist: a person who studies ancient bones and objects
Leader: a person who leads others, such as a chief or the head of a group
Hunter: a person who hunts, a person who kills animals for food

CHAPTER 17   What Will Happen to the *Titanic?*

Skimming, page 206

1. It was thought to be unsinkable, a marvel of modern engineering, a floating palace.
2. The ship sank.

Scanning for Descriptive Details, page 209

1. Clean, thick carpets, clean linens, a dining room lined with rich wooden paneling, elevators to carry people from deck to deck, a swimming pool, and a squash court.

2. The *Titanic* hit an iceberg.
3. "The ship is going to sink in an hour to an hour and a half."
4. **a.** He is stunned. **b.** There are not enough lifeboats for everyone aboard. **c.** He tells the radio operator to send out a series of distress calls.
5. They thought nothing was wrong.
6. The passengers started to panic when the *Titanic* took on a severe downward angle.
7. The *Titanic* sank, and of the more than 2,200 people aboard, only 705 were saved.

Note-taking: Chronology of Events, page 210

(sample notes) **2.** Fred Fleet, the lookout, sees something straight ahead / yells "Iceberg right ahead"
3. Thomas Andrews, the ship builder, finds water pouring into mail room / forward hold and two boiler rooms **4.** tells Captain Smith "the ship is going to sink in an hour to an hour and a half," etc.

Skimming, page 212

1. They looked for the debris trail, not the ship. **2.** They found it on September 1, 1985.

Scanning for Descriptive Details, page 214

1. It sank 12,500 feet.
2. Because a wound was opened in the starboard (right) side of the ship and water rushed into the forward compartments, which caused the ship to sink at the bow.
3. As the stern began to rise into the air, it created stress on the weaker midsection of the ship; the central part could not support the full weight of the stern.
4. The objects fell into the ocean and began a free fall to the bottom.
5. The ocean currents swept the objects away—the lighter the object, the farther it was swept. Some items fell through the surface currents in a few minutes. Many objects lingered on the currents longer. By the time all of the objects came to rest on the bottom, they created a trail of debris more than one mile long.
6. The team looked for the debris trail.
7. They began to search in the area where the *Carpathia*, the first rescue ship to arrive, had picked up the *Titanic*'s lifeboats.
8. They lowered *Argo*, the towed camera system, more than two miles and began a series of long lines running east to west, perpendicular to the trail of debris they were looking for. As they completed each line they turned north for one mile before turning back to the east to begin another long search line.

Note-taking: Chronology of Events, page 215

(sample notes) **2.** giant stern began to rise/creating stress in midsection/ship split in half **3.** objects poured into the sea/began a free fall to the bottom **4.** ocean currents swept objects away/the lighter the object the farther it swept, etc.

Using Context Clues, page 218

1. c **2.** d **3.** e **4.** f **5.** h **6.** g **7.** i **8.** a **9.** j **10.** b

Descriptive Language, page 219

(sample answers) higher/taller; greatest/most important or biggest; thick/the opposite of *thin;*
wonderful / fantastic, great; chilly/cold; severe/serious; louder/noisier; chilling/fearful;
successful/winning; giant/very big; weaker/less strong; large/big; tremendous/enormous;
lighter/less heavy; valuable/costly; small/tiny; heavier/weighing more; gigantic/very big, giant

CHAPTER 18   The Anasazi: Why Did They Leave?

Using Illustrations to Understand Ideas, page 220

1. A   **2.** A   **3.** A   **4.** C   **5.** D   **6.** B   **7.** B   **8.** D

Predicting, page 222

1. In what part of the world the Anasazi lived
2. What the people who discovered the cliff dwellings found
3. Description of the daily life of the Anasazi in the past
4. Description of the Anasazi today

Scanning to Get the Facts, pages 223–227

Paragraph A
1. It is in the southwest part of the United States.
2. The top of the mesa is covered with green plants and trees.
3. It is generally dry.
4. It comes from the winter snowfall and spring and summer rains.
5. Its purpose is to preserve and protect the culture of the Anasazi people.
6. More than 800,000 people from all over the world visit this area.

Paragraph B
1. The Anasazi lived there hundreds of years ago, between the sixth and the fourteenth centuries (A.D. 500–1300).
2. The trade center was in the Four Corners area: the states of Utah, Colorado, New Mexico, and Arizona.
3. Americans first explored this area in the early 1870s.
4. The ranchers found ruins of a great civilization: magnificent houses made out of stone under the cliffs of the canyons, pottery, baskets, wall art, and tools made from stone.
5. **a.** They were amazed and overwhelmed by the beauty of what they had found.   **b.** They asked themselves: Who had lived there and why had these people built homes in the steep canyons? How did these people survive? Why did the people abandon their cliff dwellings?

Paragraph C
1. About 600 dwellings have been found.
2. They were built during the years 1100–1300 A.D.
3. **a.** They were cut into the ground so that people entered from above.   **b.** They were used for religious worship.
4. They were very important because every building had a kiva.

Paragraph D
1. Bow and arrows and simple knives for hunting made out of wood and stone were used.
2. **a.** They made beautiful baskets and pottery covered with distinctive black geometric designs.
   b. They used the items to carry and cook food and water.
3. Their diet was simple: they ate corn, beans, squash, meat from deer and bighorn sheep, berries and other plants.
4. They moved because life in the cliff dwellings was difficult.
5. **a.** The rooms were cold and damp in the winter.   **b.** It was hard to get in and out of their homes.
6. Most Anasazi were under 5 feet tall and lived only into their twenties or thirties; the bodies found show that they had arthritis, tooth decay, broken bones, and lung disease.

Paragraph E
1. They were better built and could be defended more easily.
2. They left between the years 1200 and 1300.
3. The mystery remains about what happened to make the Anasazi leave their homes forever.

Finding the Main Ideas, page 228

Paragraph B: The discovery of Mesa Verde and its significance.
Paragraph C: Description of Mesa Verde
Paragraph D: Daily life in Mesa Verde
Paragraph E: The mystery of Mesa Verde

Word Forms, page 231

1. drawings (N)
2. dwellings (N)
3. climbing (N)
4. survival (N)
5. combination (N)
6. protect (V)
7. visitors (N)
8. abandon (V)
9. produce (N)
10. reduction (N)

Jigsaw Sentences, page 232

1. d   2. e   3. c   4. f   5. b   6. a

Possibility, page 232

(sample sentences) **1.** *Might:* Also their farming methods might have caused more food problems. If this fighting grew too intense or too difficult, then the Anasazi might have decided to abandon the canyons.
1. I think I might have a cold.
2. *Could:* This climbing . . . very dangerous for young children who could fall easily. They had moved into dwellings that could hold a number of families.
3. *Would:* This climbing would have been difficult. . . In times of famine. . . it is easy to imagine that fighting would start.